The
VIX Trader's
Handbook

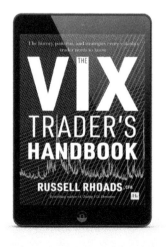

The
VIX Trader's
Handbook

The history, patterns,
and strategies every volatility
trader needs to know

Russell Rhoads

HARRIMAN HOUSE LTD
3 Viceroy Court
Bedford Road
Petersfield
Hampshire
GU32 3LJ
GREAT BRITAIN
Tel: +44 (0)1730 233870

Email: enquiries@harriman-house.com
Website: harriman.house

First published in 2020.

Hardback ISBN: 978-0-85719-711-5
eBook ISBN: 978-0-85719-712-2

British Library Cataloguing in Publication Data
A CIP catalogue record for this book can be obtained from the British Library.

CONTENTS

ABOUT
THE AUTHOR

RUSSELL RHOADS is a highly regarded strategist, educator and consultant—among other things he is perhaps best known as the author of *Trading VIX Derivatives*, the textbook in the volatility space. He works for EQDerivatives and is a clinical professor of finance at Loyola University in Chicago.

Russell spent a decade at CBOE, including a stint as director of education at The Cboe Options Institute. He has a 25-year career, which includes buyside firms such as Balyasny Asset Management, Caldwell & Orkin, and Millennium Management.

Russell is pursuing a PhD from Oklahoma State University.

INTRODUCTION

I N 2009 I became an instructor for the Options Institute at what was the Chicago Board Options Exchange (now Cboe Global Markets). None of the other instructors were paying much attention to VIX as the volume had not really taken off.

I decided to immerse myself in all things VIX. This was impeccable timing on my part as the markets were starting to emerge from the depths of the Great Financial Crisis. This was a period where VIX was front and center in the financial press as a quantification of how much fear there was in the markets.

My focus on VIX led to courses being developed at the Options Institute to specifically focus on using VIX as a market indicator, but also strategies associated with VIX futures and option contracts. Shortly before I joined Cboe, the first two exchange-traded notes based on the performance of VIX futures contracts were introduced. Although this was not a Cboe-specific market or product, I felt that focusing on and promoting these other methods of gaining exposure to the market's expectations for volatility was good for the emergence of volatility as a tradable asset. Another part of my becoming an authority on VIX involved writing a book. If you want to learn about something, write a book, it definitely will make you an expert.

My first book on VIX, *Trading VIX Derivatives*, is now a decade old. In 2009, when I wrote the book, average daily VIX futures volume was 32,000 and average daily VIX option volume was 132,000. In 2019, these average daily volume totals had increased to 248,000 and 502,000 respectively. Also, there were only two exchange-traded products available back in 2009 (VXX and VXZ). There are now 10 actively traded volatility-linked ETPs (exchange-traded products) in the US, a number that was in the mid-20s at its peak. It is an understatement to say that things have changed a bit since I wrote that first VIX book. I will also fully admit I have learned a lot over the past decade.

This book tries to appeal to all levels of market participants, from those that want to just have an understanding of how VIX and the related trading products behave, to those that may want to hedge equity exposure or take advantage of the persistent overpricing of option volatility. Also, I try to be very modular in the way I present material, which means if you are thinking about trading VIX ETPs you can jump straight to Chapter 3. If shorting a volatility spike is your area of interest, you can turn directly to Chapter 7.

HOW THIS BOOK IS STRUCTURED

This book is divided into three parts.

Part I consists of five chapters which discuss the basics of VIX, the various related trading instruments, and some markets where exposure to other volatility indexes can be traded. Chapter 5 takes a deep dive into historical price action of VIX.

Part II, covering Chapters 6 to 10, discusses the trade construction process and the various strategies that volatility traders implement in order to gain both short and long exposure to VIX.

Part III, Chapter 11, is a history lesson discussing volatility events stretching all the way back to the 1987 crash.

PART I

CHAPTER 1

Offers a brief introduction to VIX, what it is telling us and a high-level look at how it is calculated. There's also a little on why VIX has an inverse relationship with the S&P 500.

CHAPTER 2

Introduces VIX options and futures, which trade at the Cboe option exchange and Cboe futures exchange respectively. Their unique price behavior is introduced, along with an explanation of why the futures trade independently of spot VIX.

CHAPTER 3

This chapter covers the variety of volatility-related ETPs that are available for trading. This has been an area of controversy in the financial markets, mostly due to a misunderstanding of what these products offer. Despite the misunderstandings and constant bashing, as I write this the largest ETN (exchanged-traded note) based on AUM (VXX) has about $730 million in assets under management with over $2 billion invested in the variety of volatility-linked ETPs.

CHAPTER 4

Introduces tradable volatility markets that exist alongside VIX. The number two market in the volatility space is VSTOXX, which is the expected volatility of the Euro STOXX 50 index as indicated by options trading on that market. A very accurate short name for this market is the European VIX.

CHAPTER 5

A quantitative history lesson on VIX. Many market participants have short memories or have not been in the investment business long enough to fully recall VIX during periods of high or low volatility regimes. Additionally, this chapter looks at VIX versus the futures contracts, as well as how well the ETPs react relative to VIX and S&P 500 price action.

PART II

CHAPTER 6

When planning a derivative trade there are many moving parts. This is accentuated in the VIX world as the initial underlying is the S&P 500, then we look to VIX, then to the current anticipation that is present in VIX futures. Planning a VIX-related trade and choosing the best method to implement an outlook is a process that differs from most other markets. This chapter lays out what to consider before pulling the trigger.

CHAPTER 7

The first of two chapters that address being short volatility. The first look at being short volatility addresses consistent methods of taking advantage of the volatility risk premium that is available from VIX-related trading products.

CHAPTER 8

This second chapter on being short volatility addresses taking the other side of volatility spikes and how this has worked in the past. Selling into a volatility spike can be a white-knuckle experience for traders, but as with any very risky prospect, this can be a rewarding trading method.

CHAPTER 9

Shorting volatility is what the majority of professionals think of with respect to VIX. However, the headlines associated with VIX are often related to the large moves that accompany a drop in the stock market. Being long volatility is a costly venture if it does not work out perfectly, but there are still effective means for being long volatility that can be implemented at a reasonable price.

CHAPTER 10

This final chapter on trading strategies addresses spread trading between different VIX futures expirations as well as trading VSTOXX futures versus VIX. Using options and even ETPs based on the same sort of outlook is addressed as well.

PART III

CHAPTER 11

Presents a detailed analysis of a series of historic volatility events, looking back to the price history we have for VIX and its predecessor VXO.

These events include:

- Stock market crash, 1987
- Russian financial crisis, 1998
- September 11, 2001 terrorist attacks
- Great Financial Crisis, 2007–2009
- Flash crash, May 6, 2010
- European sovereign debt crisis, 2011
- Black Monday, 2015
- Brexit referendum, 2016
- Election of Donald Trump, 2016
- Global pandemic, 2020

There are lessons to be learned from these events about the market as well as what VIX does when a large amount of uncertainty enters the market.

FINAL NOTE

There are two things I do not address in this book, both of which are fairly controversial. These are:

1. The VIX settlement process.

2. Periods where traders believe VIX has been manipulated.

Cboe spells out the VIX settlement process at www.cboe.com/vix and I believe it is a transparent and consistent process. The final settlement price for open positions in VIX options and futures is based on opening prices for SPX options on the day of settlement. This is commonly referred to as AM settlement. If you are concerned about the AM settlement process, exit your VIX trades before expiration (this is what I do).

As for manipulation, I've always had a hard time seeing how this is possible for such a widely traded market, but there are always those out there who believe someone is behind the curtain controlling things to their own benefit.

My hope is that you find this book useful and it helps with your own trading strategies. I'm always open to suggestions about digging into the numbers and can be found on Twitter @RussellRhoads. Anytime I do something new or have a thought about VIX or market volatility, that's where I go to share it.

PART I

INSTRUMENTS AND MARKETS

1
IMPLIED VOLATILITY AND OPTION PRICING

THE CBOE Volatility Index or VIX is a measure that depicts the market's expectations for volatility over the next 30 calendar days. VIX is determined using the volatility expectations of a wide number of S&P 500 (SPX) index options, so it is worth going over the basics of option pricing and implied volatility. After doing that, Chapter 1 goes on to look at the inverse relationship with the S&P 500 and the S&P 500 put/call ratio.

OPTION PRICING FACTORS

The price of an option is determined by the marketplace. If there is more buying pressure, the price of an option rises. And if there is more selling pressure, the price of an option drops. Although the structure of an option is more complex than a stock or exchange-traded fund (ETF), the price discovery that occurs on an exchange is basically the same.

Option pricing models allow us to determine the theoretical price for an option based on a handful of factors. Underlying price, strike price, interest rates, dividends, time to expiration, and volatility are the inputs used in pricing models. An option pricing model allows us to solve any of those variables if we know the price of an option.

When you look at a quote screen and see an implied volatility or volatility number next to the option price, that figure has been backed into using the current market price of an option. VIX works the same way, but with many more options being used to come up with a measure of volatility expectations.

VIX CALCULATION

VIX is a measure of expected volatility that is determined using a wide number of SPX index options. The measure that results is the expected volatility from the market over the next 30 days. The specific options that are used to calculate VIX will change continuously, as only out-of-the-money calls and puts contribute to the calculation. Two different expirations contribute to the VIX calculation: the Friday before and the Friday just after the 30-day time frame that VIX was created to measure.

There are two great resources for those that would like to take a deep dive into the VIX calculation. Cboe Global Markets offers a white paper which may be found at www.cboe.com/vix. Also, for those who really want to get a feel for how VIX is calculated I would recommend the 2007 paper "Calculating VIX in Excel," by Tom Arnold and John Earl, which may be found at on SSRN.

VIX ENHANCEMENTS

What is known as VIX has undergone a few enhancements since the 1993 introduction. The first iteration of VIX was based on S&P 100 index (OEX) option pricing. Cboe maintains this index using the ticker VXO and this measure is used later in the book when discussing the history of volatility.

What is great about VXO is that it has data going back to 1986 which incorporates the price action from 1987. Back then, the VXO calculation did not take as many index options into account as the calculation of VIX does today. Since the history for VXO covers the period of the 1987 stock market crash, we have a rough idea of what the option volatility reaction was to this major market event.

Figure 1.1 is a daily chart of VXO closing prices from 1987.

Figure 1.1: Daily VXO pricing (1987)

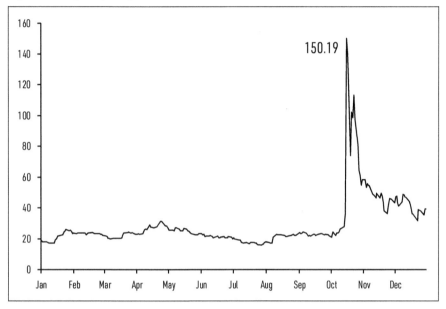

Data source: Cboe Global Markets.

On October 19, 1987 VXO closed at 150.19. Yes, that is correct. This is an interesting comparison to 2008, when the highest VIX close came in at 80.86.

Figure 1.2 presents a direct comparison of VXO during the second half of 1987 and VIX during the second half of 2008.

Figure 1.2: Daily VXO pricing 2H1987 vs. daily VIX pricing 2H2008

Data source: Cboe Global Markets.

Later in this book, Chapter 11 spends time discussing the various volatility events. Where applicable, we look at how VIX and related trading vehicles reacted leading up to, during, and after these different periods of market turmoil. The market reactions in late 1987 and 2008 will be expanded on as well. However, note the different price behavior of each in Figure 1.2.

The lighter line, which represents VXO price action, reacts very quickly and violently to the price action of October 1987. There's very little warning of the impending stock market crash and corresponding spike in index option volatility.

2008 was a different story. Bear Sterns had been absorbed by JP Morgan Chase in March of that year and rumors were rampant that other large institutions were near collapse. The move in 2008 represents a spike that occurred when the market was already expecting turbulence. In 1987, it came seemingly out of nowhere.

The reaction of broad-based index volatility to a drop in the underlying equity market has a component of surprise as well as fear to it. The 1987 versus 2008 contrast is a great illustration of this.

VIX AND THE S&P 500 RELATIONSHIP

Most people recognize VIX due to the inverse relationship that VIX has relative to the S&P 500. On days where the S&P 500 is under pressure, VIX often moves up at a magnitude that is much greater than the drop in the S&P 500.

Table 1.1 shows the 10 largest drops in the S&P 500 between 1990 and June 2020, along with the corresponding move in VIX.

Table 1.1: 10 biggest S&P 500 losses and VIX changes (1990–2018)

Date	S&P 500 change	VIX change
3/16/2020	−11.98%	42.99%
3/12/2020	−9.51%	40.02%
10/15/2008	−9.03%	25.61%
12/1/2008	−8.93%	23.93%
9/29/2008	−8.81%	34.48%
10/9/2008	−7.62%	11.11%
3/9/2020	−7.60%	29.85%
10/27/1997	−6.87%	34.31%
8/31/1998	−6.80%	11.82%
11/20/2008	−6.71%	8.89%
Average	**−8.39%**	**26.30%**

Data source: Yahoo Finance.

When the S&P 500 rallies, VIX tends to drop. Table 1.2 shows the 10 biggest gains by the S&P 500 from 1990 to June 2020, along with the corresponding change in VIX. Note that VIX dropped when the S&P 500 rallied, but not quite in the same magnitude that VIX rose when there was a big drop in the S&P 500.

The average of the 10 biggest gains in the S&P 500 is 8.12%, while the average of the 10 biggest losses is −8.39%.

The big difference is in the VIX changes over those days. On strong S&P 500 days the average drop for VIX is –11.19%, while on those very weak S&P 500 days the average gain for VIX was 26.30%.

Table 1.2: 10 biggest S&P 500 gains and VIX changes (1990–2018)

Date	S&P 500 change	VIX change
10/13/2008	11.58%	–21.39%
10/28/2008	10.79%	–16.36%
3/24/2020	9.38%	0.13%
3/13/2020	9.29%	–23.37%
3/23/2009	7.08%	–5.80%
4/6/2020	7.03%	–3.33%
11/13/2008	6.92%	–9.98%
11/24/2008	6.47%	–10.97%
3/10/2009	6.37%	–10.69%
11/21/2008	6.32%	–10.13%
Average	8.12%	–11.19%

Data source: Yahoo Finance.

This is just one example of the behavior of VIX. There is an old Wall Street saying that the stock market takes the stairs up and the elevator down. It is not too much of a stretch to say VIX takes the stairs down but rises like it was shot out of a cannon.

CBOE SPX PUT/CALL RATIO

VIX is calculated using both SPX call and put pricing.

On an average trading day, 175 SPX puts trade for each 100 SPX call options. Cboe Global Markets maintains a put to call ratio based on the SPX put and call volume each day. When there are 175 puts traded for every 100 calls, the put to call ratio would be 1.75.

Figure 1.3 shows the S&P 500 put to call ratio for all of 2018. Note the line rarely dips below 1.00, which would indicate a day where more SPX calls than puts have traded.

Figure 1.3: S&P 500 index option daily put to call ratio (2018)

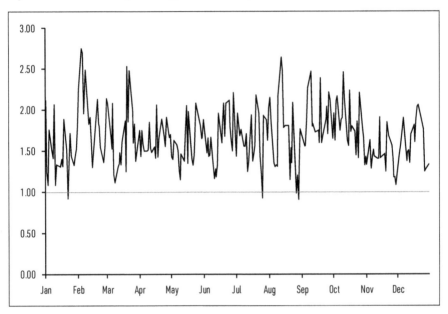

Data source: Cboe Global Markets.

Because the put side of the market does more volume, it is commonly thought that SPX put trading activity drives the price changes in VIX. This is debatable, as there is not much of a relationship between the SPX put to call ratio and price changes for VIX.

However, using data from 2011 to 2018, the average SPX put to call ratio was 1.75. For the top 10% of changes for VIX over that time period, the average SPX put to call ratio was just under 2.00. There isn't a daily relationship between the two, but on days where VIX rallies, the average SPX put volume relative to SPX call volume is usually elevated.

SUMMARY

- The level for VIX is calculated using the implied volatility of SPX option contracts.

- VIX disseminates the market's expectation for volatility over the following 30 days.

- The VIX calculation methodology has been enhanced over time and now uses SPX options expiring just before and after 30 days.

- VXO was the predecessor to VIX and has a data history back to 1986.

- VIX and the S&P 500 historically have an inverse relationship.

- The price action for VIX is driven mainly by SPX put option activity.

2

VIX FUTURES AND OPTIONS PRICE BEHAVIOR

C BOE GLOBAL Markets introduced VIX futures in 2004 through the Cboe Futures Exchange (CFE). The VIX futures market was the first to offer direct exposure to volatility. A phrase that is often used to describe the resulting market segment is *volatility as an asset class*. My preference is *volatility as a tradable asset*. Regardless of the terminology, Cboe ushered in a new tool for traders and investors to gain exposure to the market's expectations for volatility.

In 2006, the Cboe Options Exchange introduced VIX Options. VIX futures volume was sluggish prior to the introduction of VIX Options. Cross trading between the two markets was the first step toward the acceptance of volatility as a tradable asset and strong volume growth for both VIX futures and options.

After the increase in VIX futures and options volume, volatility-linked exchange-traded products (ETPs) were launched in early 2009. This chapter discusses the price behavior of VIX futures and options, while the following chapter discusses the ETPs.

VIX FUTURES

I would suggest visiting the Cboe website (www.cfe.cboe.com) to learn more about VIX futures contract specifics, such as trading hours and expiration dates. In this book, the purpose is to demonstrate the price behavior of VIX futures contracts relative to spot VIX, along with how these contracts behave as expiration date approaches.

THE VIX INDEX CANNOT BE REPLICATED

An initial point that needs to be emphasized is that the performance of the spot VIX index is impossible to replicate in a portfolio. The VIX calculation is a time weighting of two different S&P 500 index option series, which is consistently being updated. Additionally, only actively traded out-of-the-money SPX options are used in the VIX calculation.

Since the weighting of the option prices that are used to calculate VIX is constantly changing—and since some options are added to or removed from the calculation based on market conditions—replicating VIX in a portfolio would involve a tremendous amount of trading.

Finally, the option price used to calculate VIX is the midpoint of bid–ask spread. This is a price that a trader would not necessarily get filled at if they were to enter a limit order. Basically, VIX is impossible to replicate.

THERE IS NO ARBITRAGE RELATIONSHIP

Since the spot VIX performance may not be replicated in a portfolio, there is not an arbitrage relationship between spot VIX and VIX futures. This is a very important point that impacts VIX options and ETPs as well.

An example of a market that has an arbitrage relationship is the S&P 500 index and S&P 500 futures. If the S&P 500 futures rise rapidly relative to the S&P 500 index, traders may short the futures and buy a portfolio of stocks that replicates the S&P 500. When the two prices revert back to a normal spread, this trade would be unwound for a profit. This sort of potential trading is why the S&P 500 futures pricing closely tracks the spot S&P 500 index. Arbitrage firms engage in trades that keep the S&P 500 index and futures in line with each other. Since the same trading opportunity is not present in the VIX arena, VIX futures pricing may deviate relative to spot VIX.

VIX futures prices are typically at a premium relative to spot VIX. The two prices will converge at expiration, but often deviate based on a variety of market factors.

VIX AND VIX FUTURES RELATIONSHIP

In Chapter 1, we saw that VIX can rally quickly, especially when the stock market reacts to unanticipated negative news. If a trader chooses to short a VIX futures contract, they are taking on the risk that VIX and the specific contract may rally, leaving them with a significant trading loss.

This is why VIX futures are often at a premium relative to spot VIX—traders receive a premium for taking on the risk of being short a VIX future. The risk premium is most often present when VIX is at the lower end of the historical range and when there is very little time remaining until a VIX futures contract expires.

Figure 2.1 is a very generic picture of what the relationship between VIX and VIX futures looks like on the majority of trading days.

Figure 2.1: VIX in contango

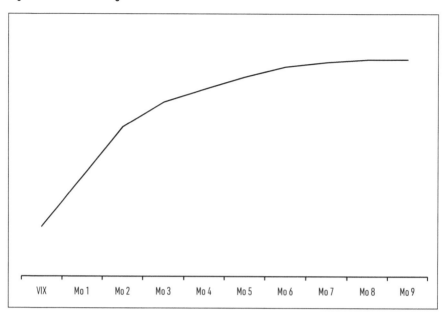

Note spot VIX is lower than all the futures depicted on this chart. Also, note that the farther out into the future, the flatter the curve. This is very typical of how the VIX term structure appears in periods of low volatility.

There are also periods of time where spot VIX is at a premium relative to VIX futures contract prices. This is often during periods when VIX is elevated. Option implied volatility is a mean reverting measure. VIX rallies quickly, but often reverts to lower levels over the course of a few days or weeks, depending on market expectations. When VIX rallies, traders have been conditioned to expect the index to revert to lower levels. The more time to expiration for a VIX futures contract, the more likely spot VIX is going to move to a lower price level.

Figure 2.2 shows VIX in what is commonly referred to as backwardation.

Figure 2.2: VIX in backwardation

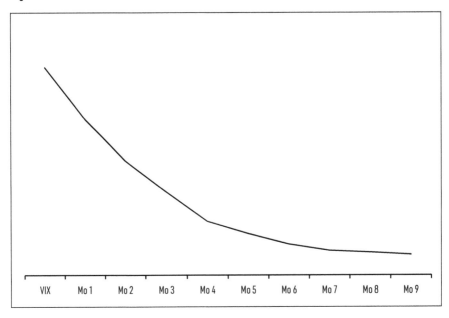

In Figure 2.2, spot VIX is elevated relative to the futures and the farther out in time, the flatter the curve. Basically, this is an instance where the VIX futures market is expecting VIX to revert to lower levels.

The chart in Figure 2.3 is a good example of the historical price relationship between VIX futures and the underlying spot VIX index. The lighter line shows the daily settlement price for the Dec 2018 VIX future and the darker line represents spot VIX closing prices for the final three months of life for the December contract.

Figure 2.3: Daily Dec 2018 VIX and VIX index pricing

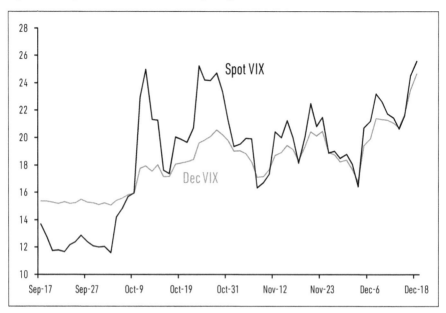

Data source: Cboe Global Markets.

The first few data points in Figure 2.3, starting from the left, were recorded with spot VIX at historically low levels. The December contract, which had several weeks remaining to expiration, is little changed each day, closing around 15.

Following this period of relative calm, VIX experiences several moves to the upside. Note that initially the December contract moves up, but not to the extent of spot VIX. This is because VIX has historically moved up quickly and given up those gains in a short period of time. When VIX futures have several weeks or months remaining to expiration, they tend to not react in lockstep with spikes in the spot VIX index.

Toward the end of Figure 2.3, spot VIX is still spiking, but notice that with very little time remaining to expiration, the futures contract is not mirroring the move in VIX. The lack of time remaining to settlement means the chances of VIX moving back to lower levels has decreased, so the futures prices follow the spot closely.

Another takeaway here, which is discussed in Chapter 4, is that the nearest expiring futures contract gives traders the very close exposure to spot VIX.

Finally, understanding the price behavior of VIX futures is key to success in trading any of the relative markets, as both option and ETP pricing is driven by VIX futures activity.

VIX OPTIONS

The basic contract specifications of VIX options are best covered on the Cboe website (www.cboe.com/vix). This section introduces VIX options from a price behavior perspective.

There are both standard monthly and weekly VIX options that are available for trading and these products share their expiration date with a corresponding VIX future. This is important to understand with respect to VIX option price behavior.

The primary thing to know about VIX options is that they are priced off the same anticipatory pricing that impacts VIX futures. Stated a little differently, the best underlying pricing to use for a VIX option is not spot VIX, but the future that shares an expiration date.

Table 2.1 shows a sample of VIX option pricing from Friday August 12, 2016, when spot VIX was trading at 11.50 and the September 2016 VIX future was trading at 15.00.

Table 2.1: September 2016 VIX option pricing

Call bid	Call ask	Strike	Put bid	Put ask
4.90	5.10	10	0.00	0.05
3.90	4.10	11	0.00	0.05
3.10	3.30	12	0.15	0.20
2.40	2.55	13	0.45	0.55
1.90	2.05	14	1.00	1.05
1.55	1.65	15	1.60	1.70
1.35	1.45	16	2.35	2.45
1.10	1.25	17	3.10	3.30

Data source: Cboe Global Markets.

If a novice trader were to see VIX quoted at 11.50 and the VIX Sep 12 put offered at 0.20, they would believe that there is a mispricing or even may have found an arbitrage opportunity. In fact, many novice traders walk away from VIX because they do not necessarily trust or understand the option pricing.

In this case, if a trader buys the VIX Sep 12 put for 0.20, they have the theoretical right to sell VIX at 12.00 when the underlying index is trading at 11.50. Buying the put assures a trader that they can sell VIX for a net cost of 11.80, after accounting for the 0.20 cost of the put. If they purchase the put and buy the underlying for 11.50, then they have locked in a profit of 0.30. However, there are two issues with this. First, VIX options are European style and may only be exercised upon expiration. Second, traders can't buy spot VIX.

All option pricing, after using a pricing formula, takes the future value of the underlying market into account. It is the interest rate part of these formulas that make this adjustment. For VIX options, the best forward value is the corresponding futures contract. In the case of the September VIX options in Table 2.1, the September VIX future which is trading at 15.00 is the best underlying price to analyze the current option price.

Note the pricing for the VIX Sep 15 call 1.55 x 1.65 and the VIX Sep 15 put 1.60 x 1.70. Both are basically in line with each other. This is the sort of pricing that is normally seen with the money option contracts.

Finally, what if a trader does not have access to VIX futures pricing? A neat trick is to take the VIX 10 strike call, determine the midpoint of the bid–ask spread, and then add 10.00 to it. For example, the bid–ask spread for the VIX Sep 10 Call is 4.90 x 5.10, so the midpoint is 5.00. 5.00 plus 10.00 results in 15.00, which is the price of the VIX September future. This back of the envelope calculation is usually in line with the VIX future price, but may be off by a nickel or dime. However, it is suitable as a substitute when futures pricing is not available.

VIX PUT–CALL RATIO

In Chapter 1, the SPX put–call ratio was used to demonstrate how S&P 500 index put options dominate the trading in that arena. For VIX option trading, the put–call ratio tells a very different story. From 2007 to 2018, the average VIX put–call ratio was 0.53. This basically may be interpreted as on average twice as many VIX calls than puts trading each day. Figure 2.4 shows the daily VIX put–call ratio over the course of 2018.

Figure 2.4: Daily 2018 VIX option put-call ratio

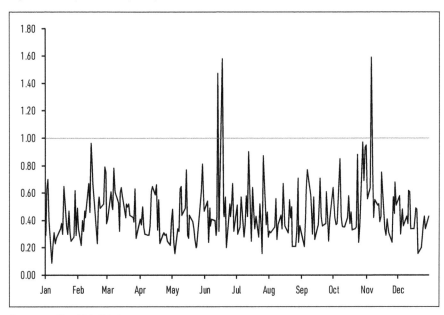

Data source: Cboe Global Markets.

The majority of observations show that many more VIX call options than put options traded on most days. For example, on February 5, 2018, 2.9 million VIX calls traded versus just over 600,000 puts. The put–call ratio for VIX is a bit more volatile than that of the S&P 500, as there are days where just a few block trades dominate the VIX volume.

Finally, there are just a few instances where more calls than puts traded in the VIX arena during 2018, but not too much should be read into that. The main takeaway here is that in the same way as SPX puts are used by traders for insuring a portfolio, VIX calls are popular for hedging, but more for hedging a quick drop in the SPX.

VIX OF VIX

The implied volatility of VIX options can be compared over time as well. Cboe actually offers a volatility index based on VIX option trading. The Cboe VVIX index (VVIX) is a measure of the expected volatility of the forward 30-day price of VIX. Note this is not an indication of the expected volatility of spot VIX. As already demonstrated, VIX option pricing is based on a forward value of VIX which is comparable to VIX futures pricing.

Cboe has historical data for VVIX dating back to January 2007. Historically, VVIX has averaged around 88. The range stretches as high as 180 and as low as just under 60. The chart in Figure 2.5 shows the annual high, low, and average for VVIX from 2007 to 2018.

Figure 2.5: VVIX high/low/average (2007–2018)

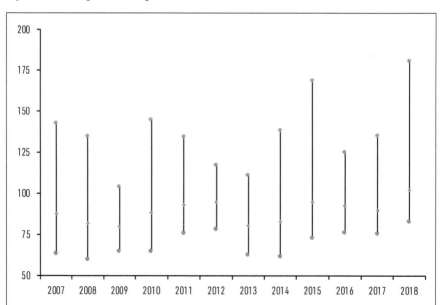

Data source: Cboe Global Markets.

The range for VVIX is typically pretty wide, as VIX option trading reacts quickly to changes in the S&P 500 and changes in VIX. When a spike occurs in VIX, call prices will naturally move up. However, due to the mean reverting nature of VIX, hedgers that have long VIX call positions on will monetize (sell) their options when VIX rallies. This is a factor that results in VVIX not necessarily rallying in line with VIX and VIX futures.

Also, when VIX is elevated, traders are often a little reluctant to purchase VIX call options as a stock market rally could quickly push VIX to lower levels. Finally, remember that the best pricing vehicle for VIX options is the corresponding VIX future. If VIX is in backwardation, that is if spot VIX is at a great premium relative to the futures contracts, call options will be much less attractive to purchase as the futures are indicating the market expects VIX to move to lower levels.

Chapter 4 spends more time on the relationship between VIX and VVIX. Chapter 11 discusses how VVIX reacted during periods of excess volatility since VIX options were introduced to the marketplace. Both are good insights into what to expect from the volatility of VIX options in different market environments.

SUMMARY

- The Cboe Futures Exchange introduced VIX futures in 2004.

- VIX options were introduced in 2006.

- Volume for VIX futures did not gain much traction until the listing of VIX options.

- The relationship between VIX and VIX futures pricing is unique due to the lack of a fair value relationship between the two.

- The best underlying pricing vehicle for VIX options is the VIX futures contract that shares an expiration date.

- VVIX or the VIX of VIX is a consistent measure of expected volatility for a 30-day forward price for VIX.

3

VOLATILITY-RELATED EXCHANGE-TRADED PRODUCTS

A THIRD TYPE of exchange-listed tradable volatility product was introduced in early 2009 in the form of the exchange-traded note (ETN). An ETN is similar to an exchange-traded fund and many traders are not even aware that most volatility-linked products use the ETN structure. Some do use the more common exchange-traded fund format (ETF). For simplicity's sake, the term exchange-traded product or ETP is used regarding general statements on these products in this chapter.

All ETPs have in common is that they do not offer direct exposure to the performance of VIX. What you get when you purchase one of these ETPs is exposure to a strategy index that dynamically holds VIX futures contracts. As previously stated, but worth re-emphasizing, direct exposure to spot VIX is costly and operationally difficult to implement. The exposure to VIX futures for each of these products is rebalanced daily and this trading action impacts the performance of these ETPs.

The iPath S&P 500 VIX Short-Term Futures ETN (VXX) was launched on January 29, 2009 and since an ETN is a bond structure it had an expiration date which was January 30, 2019. The original VXX ETN has been replaced by the iPath Series B S&P 500 VIX Short-Term Futures ETN, which is now quoted using the same ticker, VXX. The first ETN had a 10-year life, while the Series B version does not mature until January 2048.

At one time there were several volatility-related exchange-traded products that attempted to replicate the success of VXX through offering leveraged long and short exposure to VIX futures contracts. The number of ETPs has contracted and as of mid-2020 there were seven funds remaining which still offer a variety of exposure to VIX futures.

Table 3.1 offers a list and brief description of these products.

Table 3.1: Volatility-oriented ETPs

Ticker	Type	Name	Strategy
VXX	ETN	iPath Series B S&P 500 VIX Short-Term Futures ETN	Long 1st and 2nd month VIX futures
VIXY	ETF	ProShares VIX Short-Term Futures ETF	Long 1st and 2nd month VIX futures
VIXM	ETF	ProShares VIX Mid-Term Futures ETF	Long 4th to 7th month VIX futures
VXZ	ETN	iPath Series B S&P 500 VIX Mid-Term Futures ETN	Long 4th to 7th month VIX Futures
XVZ	ETN	iPath S&P 500 Dynamic VIX ETN	Dynamic allocation to short-term (VXX) and mid-term futures (VXZ) indexes
UVXY	ETF	ProShares Ultra VIX Short Term Futures	1.5x leveraged long 1st and 2nd month VIX futures
SVXY	ETF	ProShares Short VIX Short-Term Futures	0.5x short 1st and 2nd month VIX futures

Data source: Yahoo Finance.

As mentioned, some of these products are ETNs and some ETFs. The iPath products are ETNs, while the ProShares products use an ETF structure. There are four ProShares ETFs listed in the table, a couple of which have ETN counterparts. The VIXY methodology is similar to VXX's and VIXM is comparable to VXZ.

The biggest difference between the ETF and ETN structures is that an ETF will need to hold the underlying securities while an ETN will not. A secondary difference is that the ETN is a bond obligation of the firm that issues the ETN. In the unlikely event that the ETN issuer goes bankrupt, the result would be holders of the ETN having the same rights as other bondholders.

ROLL YIELD

Anyone involved in trading volatility-related ETPs should have at least a basic understanding of how rebalancing works for the strategy that the product was created to replicate.

For short-term focused ETPs, the strategy involves exposure to the first two-month volatility futures contracts. The weighting of the holdings is based on targeting a 30-day time frame. In order to maintain a 30-day exposure, the near month future weighting moves lower each day and the second month future's weighting increases. An issue here is that the two futures contract prices are rarely the same. In fact, more often than not, the front month is trading at a discount to the second month.

UNLEVERAGED LONG SHORT-TERM ETPs

The VIX-related unleveraged long short-term ETPs give holders exposure to volatility through replicating the performance of a portfolio that holds the front two monthly VIX futures contracts. The weighting in the two futures contracts is balanced to be the equivalent of holding a 30-day futures contract. The method used to do so involves holding the front two monthly futures contracts and constantly rebalancing that position each day. The rebalancing trade involves selling the front month future and buying some of the second month future. The issue with this is that on a majority of trading days the near month future is at a discount to the second month future so when the strategy behind this index rebalances for the day, lower priced futures are being sold and higher priced futures are being purchased. The performance lag that results from this trading is referred to as "negative roll yield".

The two unleveraged long short-term ETPs that offer VIX exposure are VXX and VIXY. They have their own unique indexes which perform very closely in line with each other. For price analysis purposes I have used the S&P 500

VIX Short Term Futures Index Total Return price history. Even though the original ETP, VXX, was created in early 2009, there is actually data for this index going back to before 2007 which offers a glimpse into how these three ETPs would have reacted to the Great Financial Crisis of 2008–2009.

The price behavior of the unleveraged ETPs does correlate to a degree with spot VIX. Using data from late 2007 to 2018 the beta of daily price changes for the ETPs is very close to 0.50. Market conditions vary, so I sorted beta by up and down days for spot VIX. The beta of unleveraged long ETPs is about 0.52 when VIX is higher and 0.48 when VIX is lower on the day. In general, VXX or VIXY would be expected to move about half as much as VIX does in either direction on a given day.

Price action for the three similar ETPs is represented by the daily NAV as reported by iShares for VXX. The three funds have slightly different methodologies, but the correlation of daily price changes is over 0.90 among all three. Also, VXX has a bit more history to work with than VIXY. All the figures in Table 3.2 represent price action between January 2009 and September 2019.

Table 3.2: VXX statistics (January 2009–September 2019)

Performance	Average change	Largest gain	Largest loss
Daily	−0.21%	96.11%	−25.95%
Weekly	−1.10%	46.52%	−28.28%
Monthly	−4.86%	71.16%	−32.63%

Direction	Percent positive	Percent negative	Percent unchanged
Daily	41.20%	58.24%	0.56%
Weekly	38.74%	61.26%	0.00%
Monthly	28.13%	71.87%	0.00%

Relationship	Correlation with VIX	Beta vs. VIX	Correlation S&P 500
Daily	0.90	0.51	−0.74
Weekly	0.88	0.47	−0.77
Monthly	0.85	0.64	−0.75

Data source: Bloomberg.

Since inception, VXX is down well over 99%, therefore a chart would not tell much of a story. Also, the best use for VXX, at least from the long side, is as a short-term position with the goal of benefitting from a quick drop in equity prices. The statistics in Table 3.2 demonstrate how VXX and the other unleveraged long short-term ETPs would be expected to behave over a day, week, and month along with the relationship between these ETPs, spot VIX and the S&P 500.

On average, these ETPs have lost 0.21% each day. This is mostly attributable to a negative roll yield associated with rebalancing the strategy to maintain the 30-day time frame the products were created to follow. The farther out in time, the more the average loss.

Note that the biggest daily gain is almost a doubling, at 96.11%. This is the attraction for owning a long ETP, but in order to catch a big move to the upside, the timing must be perfect. For example, of the 2,682 daily observations used to calculate Table 3.2, only five had one-day returns greater than 20%.

The beta relative to spot VIX, on a daily basis, is worth highlighting. This figure is always close to 0.50, depending on the time frame, of daily price changes. Many market participants who are new to the volatility space are perplexed when seeing VIX up much more than one of the unleveraged long ETPs on days when the stock market is selling off. This is when many investors that are new to volatility-linked ETPs get a lesson in what they really own when purchasing an ETP that offers long exposure.

UNLEVERAGED LONG MID-TERM ETPs

The second VIX-related ETP to be introduced to the market place was the iPath S&P 500 VIX Mid-Term Futures ETN (VXZ). Like with VXX, the first version of VXZ was retired in January 2019 and replaced with the iPath Series B S&P 500 VIX Mid-Term Futures ETN, which now uses the same VXZ ticker.

In addition to VXZ, the VIXM ETF is available to get long exposure to fourth through seventh month VIX futures contracts.

These two ETPs rebalance daily, but because this rebalance involves longer dated futures contracts the price impact is not as significant as it is for the unleveraged long ETPs focusing on the short end (month one and two) of the VIX futures curve. Also, exposure to longer dated futures means when spot VIX rallies, the mid-term ETPs will not react as closely to this move as the shorter dated funds.

Table 3.3: VXZ statistics (January 2009–September 2019)

Performance	Average change	Largest gain	Largest loss
Daily	−0.09%	26.55%	−8.79%
Weekly	−0.44%	21.48%	−11.86%
Monthly	−1.92%	28.81%	−18.63%

Direction	Percent positive	Percent negative	Percent unchanged
Daily	45.55%	54.23%	0.22%
Weekly	42.34%	57.66%	0.00%
Monthly	32.03%	67.97%	0.00%

Relationship	Correlation with VIX	Beta vs. VIX	Correlation S&P 500
Daily	0.81	0.20	−0.76
Weekly	0.77	0.20	−0.74
Monthly	0.74	0.27	−0.72

Data source: Bloomberg.

The largest gains over daily, weekly, and monthly time periods show how much VXZ trails the performance of both the ETPs focusing on the short end of the curve as well as spot VIX. Also, note the beta of VXZ versus VIX in Table 3.3—this figure is very low relative to the correlation between VIX and VXZ. This can be read into as VXZ moving in the same direction as VIX, but not nearly at the same magnitude as VIX's price changes.

The VXZ exposure to VIX has a very low beta of 0.20 on a daily basis, rising to 0.27 when comparing monthly price action. The less time to expiration, the more sensitive VIX futures pricing is to the spot index. This shows up when comparing the betas of VXX and VXZ relative to spot VIX.

STRATEGY-BASED ETP

There have been a handful of ETPs in the past that attempted to offer systematic exposure to a VIX-related strategy. At the time of writing, there is a single fund that offers rules-based exposure: the iPath S&P 500 Dynamic VIX ETN (XVZ).

XVZ has a rules-based process that switches between the indexes behind VXX and VXZ depending on the relative levels of volatility along the forward curve. The goal of XVZ is to minimize the negative roll yield that holders of VXX are exposed to, while also offering long exposure to volatility. The results of this strategy from January 2009 to September 2019 appear in Table 3.4.

Table 3.4: XVZ statistics (January 2009–September 2019)

Performance	Average change	Largest gain	Largest loss
Daily	−0.04%	12.86%	−6.49%
Weekly	−0.23%	11.65%	−7.47%
Monthly	−1.01%	12.56%	−11.97%

Direction	Percent positive	Percent negative	Percent unchanged
Daily	49.71%	50.00%	0.29%
Weekly	44.55%	55.45%	0.00%
Monthly	39.18%	60.82%	0.00%

Relationship	Correlation with VIX	Beta vs. VIX	Correlation S&P 500
Daily	0.41	0.05	−0.56
Weekly	0.35	0.04	−0.49
Monthly	0.48	0.07	−0.50

Data source: Bloomberg.

This strategy-oriented ETP does not grind lower in the same way VXX does, but the result is smaller large gains when some sort of volatility event pushes VIX and VIX futures to higher levels. The average daily loss is only 0.04%, but this is accompanied by the biggest gain coming in at 12.86%, much lower than that of VXX. This ETP actually has a lower correlation with VIX than other long products and the beta shows basically no real relationship at all with VIX.

A final note with respect to strategy-based VIX ETPs: Transparency rules that relate to exchange-traded products changed in 2019 and one result is an increase in the listing of actively managed ETPs. Several are planned for 2020 so this segment of the listed volatility market will be expanding.

LEVERAGED LONG ETPs

The leveraged long ETP is actually very popular among short-term traders and can also be an effective tool for getting very short-term long exposure to volatility.

UVXY gives holders 1.5x long exposure to the front two monthly VIX futures contracts. UVXY originally offered 2.0x long exposure, but reduced this figure to 1.5x after the dramatic price action in the volatility markets that occurred in February 2018. The negative roll yield that often hampers the performance of funds like VXX is accentuated for these two ETPs. That is why for a holder of a long position, a very short time frame is recommended.

Table 3.5 is a breakdown of the performance of a daily position returning 1.5 times that of VXX. This is the performance that would be expected from UVXY if it were launched in early 2009 and also offered returns equal to 1.5x the strategy behind VXX.

Table 3.5: 1.5x VXX (UVXY) statistics (January 2009–September 2019)

Performance	Average change	Largest gain	Largest loss
Daily	-0.32%	144.16%	-38.92%
Weekly	-1.71%	66.25%	-40.73%
Monthly	-7.59%	116.91%	-45.93%

Direction	Percent positive	Percent negative	Percent unchanged
Daily	41.20%	58.24%	0.56%
Weekly	37.66%	62.34%	0.00%
Monthly	24.22%	75.78%	0.00%

Relationship	Correlation with VIX	Beta vs. VIX	Correlation S&P 500
Daily	0.90	0.77	−0.74
Weekly	0.89	0.70	−0.78
Monthly	0.86	0.95	−0.75

Data source: Bloomberg.

Based on the compiled history, UVXY would be expected to lose over 7.5% in the average month and a long-term holder would lose money three out of every four months. The attraction to a levered long position holding the front two-month VIX futures contract shows up in the gain columns, where a return of well over 100% could be had in a single day.

One other interesting figure in Table 3.5 is the beta versus VIX. Note how much higher this is related to the beta for VXX, with the monthly beta for UVXY versus VIX approaching 1.00.

Note that the approach to buying leveraged long ETPs involves considering the option-like nature of these two products. If a trader purchases an out-of-the-money option contract, expecting some sort of event, they will also be aware that if the event does not happen quickly the option will start to experience time decay. Traders should have the same mentality when considering buying either UVXY or even VXX. If a quick pop in VIX and VIX futures does not happen in a short amount of time, the result will be some losses for either ETP, similar to losses associated with time decay when purchasing options.

SHORT ETPs

Before discussing the short ETPs it should be acknowledged that there was some dramatic history with respect to these products in early February 2018. The price action resulted in one short ETP closing up shop and SVXY reducing the short exposure it offered to the front two-month VIX futures contracts. The price event in February 2018 is discussed in Chapter 11, which covers some significant historical volatility events.

Currently there is just one exchange-traded product that offers short volatility exposure. SVXY now offers a short exposure of 50% to the front two-monthly VIX futures contracts.

On a daily basis, SVXY will roughly return half the inverse return for VXX. As noted above, the strategy behind SVXY was reduce inverse exposure from 100% to 50% in February 2018. For this book, a history for SVXY using the current 50% strategy was calculated to show statistics that mirror this fund's returns as if it had been around since the launch of VXX.

Table 3.6 was created using the hypothetical returns by calculating returns using half the inverse daily return for VXX. This adjusted history is used to show how the strategy SVXY now employs would have performed in the past.

Table 3.6: –0.5x VXX (SVXY) statistics (January 2009–September 2019)

Performance	Average change	Largest gain	Largest loss
Daily	0.20%	17.52%	−24.50%
Weekly	0.95%	18.93%	−15.55%
Monthly	4.15%	22.74%	−22.66%

Direction	Percent positive	Percent negative	Percent unchanged
Daily	58.24%	41.20%	0.56%
Weekly	62.52%	37.48%	0.00%
Monthly	75.78%	24.22%	0.00%

Relationship	Correlation with VIX	Beta vs. VIX	Correlation S&P 500
Daily	−0.89	−0.23	0.77
Weekly	−0.87	−0.22	0.78
Monthly	−0.85	−0.30	0.77

Data source: Bloomberg.

On average, returns are positive across all time frames measured, with an impressive 4.15% average monthly return. Of course, those returns are accompanied by some dramatic drawdowns, with the worst month consisting of a drop of 22.66%.

A final statistic worth pointing out is the high correlation of the short fund's returns with that of the S&P 500. A short volatility position is often thought of as being similar to a leveraged long position in the underlying index. This is explored further at the end of this chapter, but in Table 3.6 the correlation of SVXY to the S&P 500 is either 0.77 or 0.78 depending on the time frame.

SHORT VOLATILITY VERSUS LONG INDEX

A final note regarding the short ETNs and their respective underlying markets.

Short volatility ETPs have a high correlation with the related underlying stock market index. Due to this relationship, some market participants refer to these funds as a method of having leveraged long exposure to the corresponding index. To explore this concept, I conducted a quick study using the -.5x VXX, -1x VXZ, and S&P 500 index monthly returns that were used to calculate the tables above.

An average annual return and average annual volatility of those returns was calculated along with a Sharpe ratio for SVXY and the S&P 500. The result is pretty interesting, with SVXY outperforming the S&P 500 while taking on a much larger amount of risk. Those figures appear in Table 3.7.

Table 3.7: SVXY and S&P 500 annualized performance (January 2009–September 2019)

ETP / Index	Average annual return	Average volatility of returns	Average Sharpe ratio	Worst month
SVXY	61.97%	27.11%	2.72	−22.66%
S&P 500	12.31%	11.58%	1.37	−10.99%

Data source: Bloomberg.

SVXY offers a rolling average annual return of over 60%, which is accompanied by an average annualized volatility of those returns at 27.11%. While the average annual return for the S&P 500 over the same period of time is 12.31% with a volatility of those returns of 11.58%. Either is a good long-term strategy, but the choice may come down to an individual's risk tolerance.

All the VIX-related ETPs have their proper place in the VIX ecosystem. There is nothing wrong with owning a long ETP when there are concerns about a potential quick drop in the stock market. The short ETPs offer interesting returns that come with potentially difficult drawdowns. Throughout the rest of this book, strategies using these various products, along with options on them, will be demonstrated.

SUMMARY

- VIX ETPs do not offer direct exposure to the VIX index.

- Long VIX ETPs have performed well during historic volatility events.

- Over the long term, long VIX ETPs lose money due to VIX futures trading at a premium to spot VIX as well as a negative roll yield.

- Short VIX-related ETPs benefit from the negative roll yield and offer long-term positive returns.

- The short funds will periodically experience dramatic drawdowns. This should be considered before purchase.

4

ALTERNATIVES TO VIX-RELATED MARKETS

VIX FUTURES, options, and related ETP trading are all part of the listed volatility trading space and they are all ways to give a portfolio exposure to expected volatility. The pricing of each is closely related to each of the other methods. The presence of these various products has resulted in listed volatility having a sufficient liquidity pool to accommodate large institutional orders on a regular basis. For instance, when VIX option orders are executed, the market makers will often hedge themselves by trading the corresponding VIX future and of course rebalancing for volatility-linked ETPs creates volume in the VIX futures markets.

There have been other products launched and then delisted after they did not garner enough interest from market participants. However, there are a few that are worth discussing as they are relatively new to the marketplace or have the possibility of becoming an alternative or complement to tradable VIX products.

VSTOXX

The most viable market after VIX are the VSTOXX futures and options on VSTOXX futures. These are both listed on the Eurex Exchange. The VSTOXX index is calculated using Euro STOXX 50 Index Option pricing as the model input, in the same way that SPX option pricing is used to calculate VIX. The result is an indicator of the market's expectations for Euro STOXX 50 price volatility over the next 30 days, the same forward-looking time frame as for VIX.

VSTOXX data exists from the beginning of 1999 so there is a robust amount of observations to gain an understanding as to how VSTOXX behaves. Figure 4.1 shows the monthly high, low, and average close by month from 1999 to 2019. It is no surprise that the VSTOXX chart looks an awful lot like a VIX chart.

Figure 4.1: VSTOXX monthly price action (1999–2019)

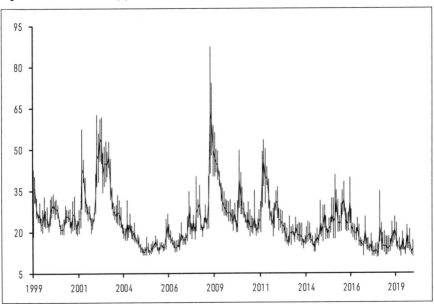

Data source: Bloomberg.

Although the chart is a mirror image of VIX price action, the levels are a bit different. The peak close for VSTOXX over this time frame is 87.51, versus 80.86 for VIX, and lowest for VSTOXX 10.68, versus 9.14 for VIX.

The VSTOXX average is 23.73, versus 19.72 for VIX. This difference is understandable as the realized volatility for the underlying markets differs as well. Average 30-day realized volatility for the Euro STOXX 50 index is 19.58%, higher than 15.71% for the S&P 500. It is worth noting that the average difference between the two volatility indexes, as well as the difference between the realized volatility of each underlying market, are both very close to 4%.

The inverse relationship that exists between VSTOXX and the Euro STOXX 50 is similar to that of VIX and the S&P 500. The correlation of daily price changes for VSTOXX and the Euro STOXX 50 is close to –0.70, while the same relationship between the S&P 500 and VIX is –0.72. This inverse relationship means that trading approaches for VIX may be applied to VSTOXX as well.

Figure 4.2 shows the daily price action for VSTOXX and the Euro STOXX 50 over the course of 2019. Again, without the numbers, this could be mistaken for a chart showing VIX and the S&P 500. The sell-offs in the Euro STOXX 50 index are accompanied by quick moves to the upside in the Euro STOXX 50.

Figure 4.2: VSTOXX vs. Euro STOXX 50 daily prices (2019)

Data source: Bloomberg.

The day-to-day price changes for VSTOXX and VIX tend to mirror each other. Often when the European markets are open and it is early in the day in the US, the US stock market will be taking European stock performance into account. The result is that when both Euro STOXX 50 and SPX markets are open, their day-to-day performance has a correlation of about +0.58. This relationship carries over to the respective volatility indexes. Figure 4.3 shows the daily price changes for both VSTOXX and VIX over the course of 2019.

Figure 4.3: VSTOXX vs. VIX daily prices (2019)

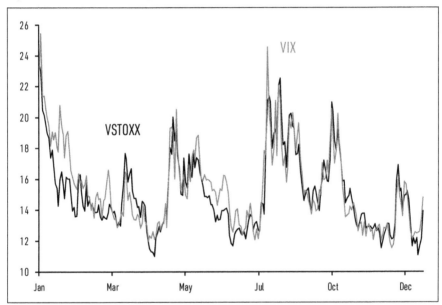

Data source: Bloomberg.

Note that both the volatility indexes move in the same direction, but there are times when they deviate from each other. This sort of price behavior lends itself to spread trading, which is discussed a little more in Chapter 10. Also, a slight difference between VSTOXX and VIX is that VSTOXX has demonstrated a bit more anticipatory behavior than VIX. This is discussed using the 2016 Brexit referendum as an example in Chapter 11.

VSTOXX DERIVATIVES

VSTOXX futures began trading at Eurex in 2009, toward the very end of the financial crisis. Average daily volume for VSTOXX futures in 2019 was about 63,000 contracts, up from about 40,000 in 2016. The VSTOXX option market has experienced growth as well, with average daily volume in 2016 at about 20,000 contracts, rising to about 30,000 in 2019.

VSTOXX and VIX have a close relationship as they are both measures of volatility expectations for broad-based indexes in developed markets. However, there have been times where the two have deviated due to issues that are more relevant to either individual market.

The biggest difference between VIX and VSTOXX futures contracts is the notional value of each contract. VIX futures have a multiplier of $1,000. Therefore, if a VIX future is priced at 20, the notional value of the contract is $20,000. VSTOXX contracts have a multiplier of €100. If a VSTOXX future is priced at 20, the notional value of a contract would be €2,000. The exact figure relationship between the two would depend on the Euro/USD exchange rate, but based on history it is roughly 10 VSTOXX to 1 VIX futures contract.

The price behavior of VSTOXX futures is very similar to the price behavior of VIX futures. Specifically, during periods of low or normal volatility the futures contracts trade at a premium to the spot index. Figure 4.4 demonstrates this using closing VSTOXX pricing on March 20, 2019.

Figure 4.4: VSTOXX index and futures pricing (March 20, 2019)

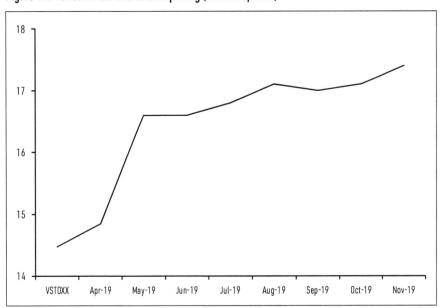

Data source: Bloomberg.

Spot VSTOXX closed at 14.48 on March 20 and the April front month future was at a slight premium at 14.85. Generally, the farther out on the curve, the higher the settlement prices for VSTOXX futures contracts. When the spot index moves up quickly, the term structure based on the spot index and futures pricing will invert. For example, the term structure chart in Figure 4.5 shows the closing VSTOXX index pricing and available futures contracts on May 9, 2019.

Figure 4.5: VSTOXX index and futures pricing (March 20, 2019)

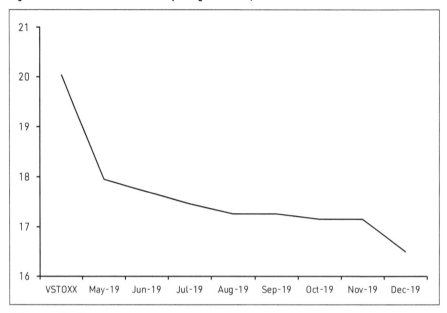

Data source: Bloomberg.

On May 9, VSTOXX rose from 17.64 to 20.04, a gain of 2.40 points or about 13.6%. The front month May future, which had about two weeks left to expiration, rose from 16.50 to 17.95, a gain of 1.45 or about 8.8%. The curve was already slightly in backwardation as market volatility had been rising for a few days before this one-day price change, but went into a well-defined state of backwardation on this move for VSTOXX above 20.

Eurex also lists VSTOXX options which have a one-to-one relationship with the corresponding VSTOXX futures contracts. They are structured as options on futures, but if held to settlement the result is a cash settlement. Before expiration, the best pricing vehicle for VIX options is the corresponding future—this holds true for VSTOXX options as well.

A final notable aspect of VSTOXX options is that they are American style, which allows a holder to exercise a long option position with the result being a long or short position in the corresponding futures contract. This contrasts with VIX options, which are European style and may not be exercised until expiration. However, both VSTOXX and VIX options do share similar underlying pricing in the form of the corresponding future; VSTOXX is just more direct about this relationship, using an option on futures structure.

SPIKES

The SPIKES index has been around since early 2016 and was originally created by the BATS Exchange as an alternative to VIX. As part of the Cboe purchase of BATS which was announced in 2016, the SPIKES index moved over to the MIAX Exchange. This index is similar to VIX, but the input for the calculation is SPY ETF options as opposed to SPX index options that are used for VIX. Also, the SPIKES index is calculated using only standard third Friday SPY options, as opposed to VIX which uses the weekly or standard SPX options that expire just before and just after the 30-day time frame that the index is charged with measuring.

There is historical data available for SPIKES going back to January 10, 2005. This history offers a robust set of data to analyze the behavior of SPIKES along with comparing this index with VIX. Figure 4.6 shows the monthly high, low, and average close for SPIKES from January 2005 through the end of 2019.

Figure 4.6: SPIKES monthly price action (2005–2019)

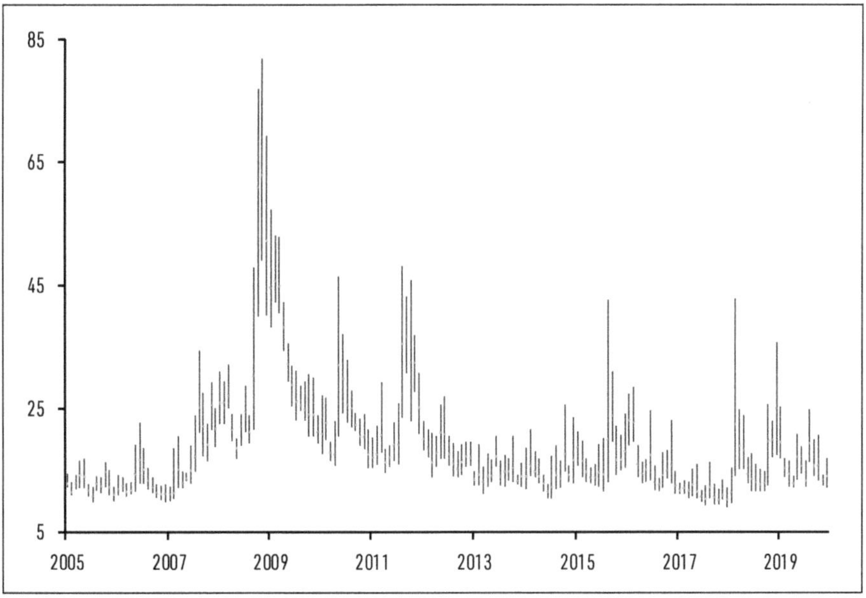

Data source: Bloomberg.

This chart could be mistaken for VIX price action by those who closely follow the volatility markets. However, the levels on a month-to-month basis are slightly different, which is a function of options on a slightly different market and different expirations being used by VIX and SPIKES to determine a 30-day expected volatility measure.

Since the SPIKES index is calculated using SPY options, the price action of SPIKES is best compared to the price changes for the SPY ETF. The long-term correlation of daily price changes for the SPIKES and SPY is −0.72, which is in line with the relationship between VIX and the S&P 500 over that time period. Figure 4.7 shows the daily price action for SPIKES and SPY in 2019.

Figure 4.7: SPIKES vs. SPY daily prices (2019)

Data source: Bloomberg.

The price behavior of SPIKES on these days where the SPY ETF was under pressure is exactly what would be expected from the volatility priced into options on the SPY. That is a rise in implied volatility due to the increased risk associated with the underlying instrument. Traditionally, the quick moves up in the SPIKES index accompany minor sell-offs in the S&P 500.

Table 4.1 displays the price reaction for the SPIKES index on the 10 worst days for the SPY ETF over the recorded history of SPIKES.

Table 4.1: SPIKES price behavior on 10 worst days for SPY (2005–2019)

Rank	Date	SPY ETF	SPIKES
1	15/10/08	−9.84%	18.90%
2	01/12/08	−8.86%	21.85%
3	29/09/08	−7.84%	36.59%
4	20/11/08	−7.42%	8.47%
5	12/11/08	−7.35%	12.05%
6	09/10/08	−6.98%	11.26%
7	08/08/11	−6.51%	47.06%
8	19/11/08	−6.41%	9.60%
9	06/11/08	−5.54%	19.79%
10	22/10/08	−5.45%	30.75%

Data source: Bloomberg.

Most of these observations occurred in 2008 and even though the market was experiencing unprecedented volatility, SPIKES gained more than the SPY lost in each of these observations.

Finally, the relationship between SPIKES and VIX is also what would be expected. That is, they track each other very closely, but not perfectly. The daily price change correlation between these two indexes is +0.98. However, the average closing price difference has SPIKES at a premium of about 0.20. Figure 4.8 shows the daily price changes for VIX and SPIKES in 2019. The lines overlap, but there are some slight differences between the two.

Figure 4.8: SPIKES vs. VIX daily (2019)

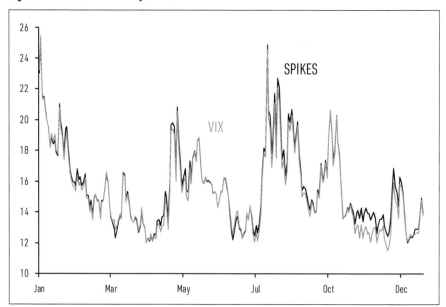

Data source: Bloomberg.

A noticeable anomaly on this price chart is the consistent premium of SPIKES relative to VIX in the November time frame (where the darker line is consistently higher than the lighter line on the right side of the chart). The average spread between the two indexes for November has SPIKES 0.95 higher than VIX. If the derivatives on each index reflect this difference, it is possible spread trading between SPIKES and VIX futures and options can present some opportunities.

The spread widening in November turns out to be a seasonal pattern that has been in place since the VIX calculation was changed to include weekly options instead of only standard third Friday of the month options. Recall that the input to SPIKES is the third Friday SPY option contracts. Figure 4.9 shows the high, low, and average spread by month as calculated by subtracting VIX from SPIKES. Data for each month from 2015 to 2019 is used to calculate these levels.

Figure 4.9: Average SPIKES minus VIX by month (2015–2019)

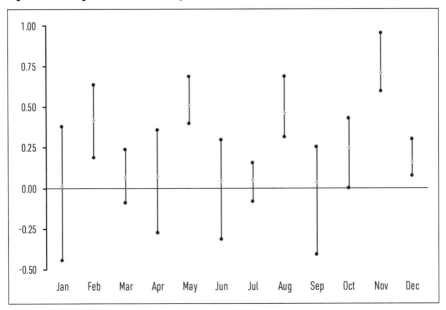

Data source: Bloomberg.

The data breaks down the relative price behavior of the SPIKES and VIX index by month. The pattern repeats every third month of the year including February, May, August, and November. Therefore, it appears that the wide spread in November of 2019 is not necessarily an anomaly, but represents a seasonal pattern that shows up in the difference between the two indexes. This relative price behavior may offer trading opportunities if it carries over to the options and futures markets based on each index.

SPIKES DERIVATIVES

Options on SPIKES began trading at MIAX in early 2019 and the trading volume has been respectable for a new product. For example, over 113,000 options on SPIKES traded in December 2019. The volume in 2019 represented a good start for this new version of gaining exposure to expected volatility. As of early 2020, there are plans for futures on SPIKES to be listed at the Minneapolis Grain Exchange to complement the option market.

RUSSELL 2000 VOLATILITY INDEX

The S&P 500 is a large cap, global index and a good counterpart to the S&P 500 is the Russell 2000, which represents small cap stocks that for the most part do business domestically in the US. Although both indexes are comprised of US stocks, very different macroeconomic trends influence the price behavior of the stocks that comprise each index. This shows up in a divergence between the price changes of the two indexes and also shows up in the behavior of implied volatility of each index.

The Russell 2000 Volatility Index (RVX) is quoted by Cboe and uses a similar methodology to VIX. A main difference between the two is only standard third Friday monthly options are used as the pricing input for RVX, and of course the underlying options are index options listed on the Russell 2000. Futures on RVX were listed for some time, but as of early 2020 are not available for trading. There are rumors RVX futures may be offered again in the future, so the index is discussed in this chapter.

RVX displays the same sort of price behavior as the other volatility indexes associated with broad-based equity market indexes. Specifically, it rises rapidly during periods of higher uncertainty associated with downside price changes in the associated index. Figure 4.10 shows the monthly high, low, and average for RVX from 2004 to 2019.

Figure 4.10: RVX monthly price action (2004–2019)

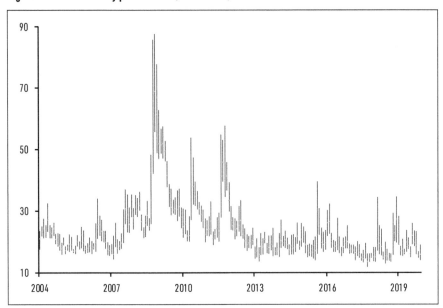

Data source: Bloomberg.

RVX reached a peak close in late 2008 of 87.62. The lowest closing price for RVX is 11.83, which was recorded in September 2017 during a period of very low volatility in the US equity markets. The average price for RVX is 23.48, which is much higher than the 18.21 for VIX over the same period of time.

The correlation of daily price changes between RVX and the Russell 2000 from 2004 to 2019 is –0.72, which is very similar to the correlation between VIX and the S&P 500 at –0.70 over the same time period. That typical inverse relationship is displayed in the price action of 2019 in Figure 4.11.

Figure 4.11: RVX vs. Russell 2000 daily prices (2019)

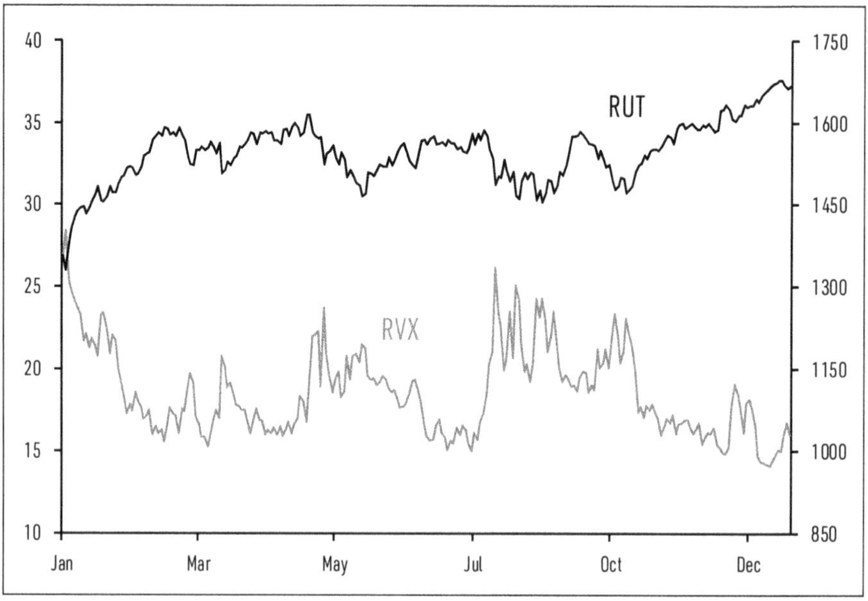

Data source: Bloomberg.

Figure 4.12 shows the daily pricing for both RVX and VIX over the course of 2019. Both volatility measures move in the same direction on most trading days. The long-term correlation of price changes between the two is about +0.90. In 2019, RVX closes at a premium to VIX each day, which is common in the RVX–VIX relationship.

Figure 4.12: RVX vs. VIX daily prices (2019)

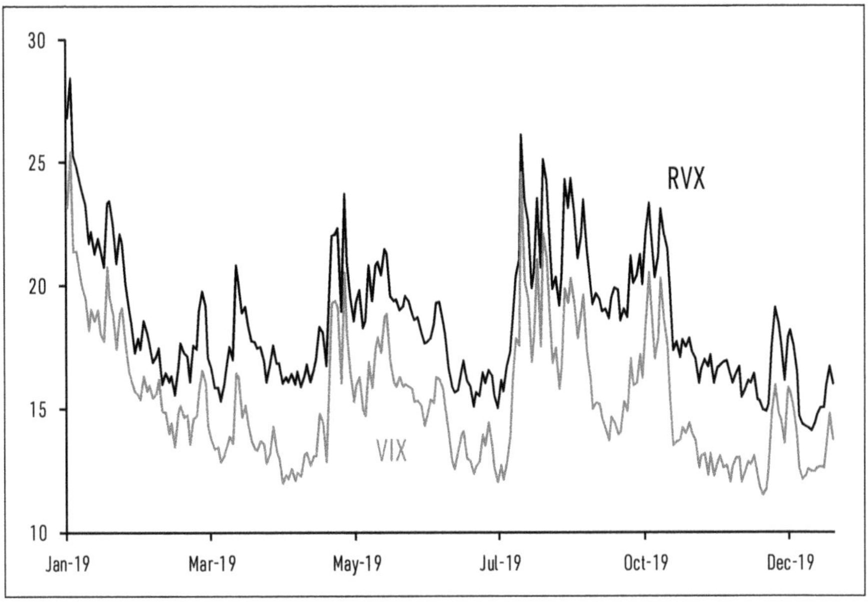

Data source: Bloomberg.

The relationship between RVX and VIX has been fairly consistent over time, with RVX consistently trading at a premium to VIX, with a few short-lived periods of time where VIX closed at a premium to RVX. The average difference between RVX and VIX has RVX at a 5.27 premium to VIX, with this spread widening to 12.84 in April 2009 for the largest RVX premium to VIX on record. In February 2018, VIX raced up to a 6.02 point premium versus RVX. This price action coincided with the volatility event early that month which is commonly referred to as *Volmageddon*—this is covered in depth in Chapter 11. Finally, of the 4,000 trading days that both VIX and RVX have been around, VIX has closed at a premium to RVX only 30 times.

SUMMARY

- VSTOXX futures and options on futures are the second most active listed volatility market after VIX.

- Many market participants refer to VSTOXX as the European Volatility Index.

- The close, but not perfect relationship between VIX and VSTOXX creates interesting spread trading opportunities.

- The SPIKES index is a measure of expected volatility over the next 30 days that uses SPY option prices in the calculation.

- There is currently no listed derivative based on the Russell 2000 Volatility Index (RVX) but this may change in the future.

5

HISTORICAL VIX STUDIES

THIS CHAPTER is intended to educate the reader on the history of VIX, VIX derivatives, and their relationship with the S&P 500. Traders who are new to the VIX-related markets will find this an initial useful lesson on just how VIX and the various vehicles that traders use to gain exposure to VIX have behaved in the past. Those that have been focusing on this market for some time will hopefully find the chapter a great refresher on how VIX has behaved in the past. Finally, this chapter takes a look at the overall history of VIX. The final chapter in this book is a history lesson as well, but only covers VIX during periods of higher market volatility.

The history of VIX goes back to 1990, while the history of VIX derivatives, including ETPs, runs from 2007 to 2018. Although VIX futures were introduced in 2004, volume did not really gain traction until 2007, so any futures-related testing starts on the first day of 2007. Also, the first ETP was not introduced until early 2009, but these products follow an index and the underlying index history stretches back before 2007.

VIX VERSUS THE S&P 500

VIX is nothing more than the market's expectation relative to future price behavior of the S&P 500. However, as noted earlier in this book and recognized by all levels of market participants, VIX has a day-to-day inverse relationship with the S&P 500. This relationship varies depending on the current market environment as well as the current level of VIX. Stated non-quantitatively, if VIX indicates the market is going to be very volatile it may not react too much when the market is volatile. And if VIX indicates the market is expected to be less volatile, if we do get high volatility, VIX adjusts accordingly.

The price behavior of VIX operates within a range. This range is pretty wide and theoretically VIX could be very close to zero or much higher than the mid-100s, a level that VXO experienced in 1987. Using data from 1990 to 2019, the all-time closing high for VIX is 80.86 (November 20, 2008) and the closing low is 9.14 (November 3, 2017). The average closing price for VIX is 19.15, but this does not mean that VIX above 19.15 is considered high and VIX below 19.15 is considered low. This is demonstrated best by looking at the distribution of VIX closing prices by handle (the figure before the decimal in the price). A histogram showing this distribution appears in Figure 5.1.

Figure 5.1: VIX closing prices by handle

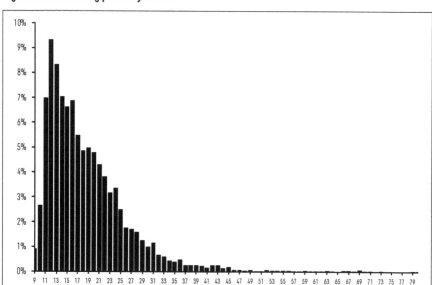

Data source: Bloomberg.

Although the long-term average for VIX is over 19, the most common closing handle for VIX is a 12, with just over 9% of closing prices. A VIX close of 17.40 is the mid-point close for VIX and is probably a more appropriate level to use to define high and low for VIX. Many market participants lean toward 16 as a sort of benchmark between what is considered high and low for VIX.

VIX is known for having an inverse relationship with the S&P 500. However, this relationship is not consistent over all time frames or market situations. In fact, VIX moves in the same direction as the S&P 500 more often than people think, it is just rare that both trend in the same direction. Table 5.1 shows the number of days the S&P 500 has been higher or lower over the 19-year period from 2000 to 2018, along with the percentage of each observation where VIX moved in the opposite direction for the day.

Table 5.1: Daily S&P 500 and VIX directional moves (2000-2019)

S&P 500 higher	VIX lower	Percent opposite
2694	2193	81.43%
S&P 500 lower	**VIX higher**	**Percent opposite**
2335	1835	78.59%

Data source: Bloomberg.

Over this 20-year period there were 5,031 trading days. The S&P 500 was higher on 2,643 of those trading days and lower on 2,335. There were three days where the S&P 500 was unchanged on the day.

When the S&P 500 rose VIX moved down 81.43% of trading days and when the S&P 500 lost value on the day VIX rose 78.59%. In rough numbers, about 20% of trading days over this period of time VIX and the S&P 500 moved in the same direction. In fact, on a percentage basis, VIX dropped more often when the S&P 500 was down than it rose when the S&P 500 moved up on the day. The main takeaway is that VIX and the S&P 500 have a negative relationship over a long period of time, but there are periods of time where they do move in line with each other. This is not necessarily something to get excited about.

Over this time period the correlation of daily price changes is about −0.72. Over shorter time periods the correlation deviates from this figure. Figure

5.2 is a chart showing the rolling 30-trading day correlation between the daily percentage price changes for the S&P 500 and VIX. Saying this is a volatile reading would be an understatement.

Figure 5.2: Rolling 30-day VIX correlation with S&P 500 by year (2000–2019)

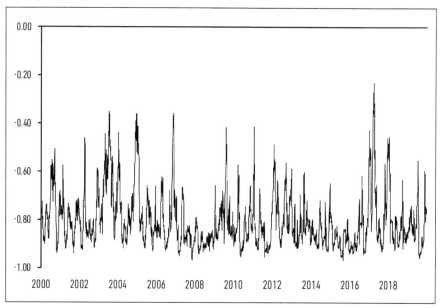

Data source: Bloomberg.

The 30-day price relationship with the S&P 500 over this period of time ranges from just under −0.20 and bordering on −1.00. The long-term average of the 30-day correlation between the daily price changes for the S&P 500 and VIX averages about −0.75. Typically, when the relationship over a shorter period of time deviates from what is expected to be the normal inverse relationship, it tends to come back to a more inverse pairing fairly quickly.

Digging a bit deeper, it appears where VIX is trading at the time will have an impact on the shorter-term correlation between VIX and the S&P 500. Table 5.2 shows the average for VIX over each 30-day correlation period and divides the observations by quartiles based on this level for VIX.

Table 5.2: Daily S&P 500 and VIX directional moves (2000–2019)

Quartile	Average VIX low	Average VIX high	Low correlation	High correlation	Average correlation
1	9.95	13.88	−0.95	−0.23	−0.77
2	13.89	17.13	−0.97	−0.39	−0.82
3	17.14	23.03	−0.97	−0.35	−0.81
4	23.04	64.99	−0.95	−0.42	−0.82

Data source: Bloomberg.

The correlation between VIX and the S&P 500 is a little less negative when VIX is at low levels. This is most likely a factor of VIX having somewhat of a floor in the low 9s. Intraday the 9 level has been violated, but the lowest close had a 9 handle. This would show up in the lack of a negative correlation because if VIX is already at the low end of the historical range it would not move down much, even if there was a big rally in the S&P 500.

VIX FUTURES

Understanding spot VIX is useful, but the real instruments that drive the VIX trading environment are the VIX futures contracts. As of the end of 2019, there are VIX futures expiring on a monthly cycle going out as much as 10 months and also VIX futures that expire on a weekly basis. The tenth month is a relatively recent addition, with the typical time frame being nine months over most of the historical period that VIX futures have been available for trading. The non-standard or Weekly VIX futures contracts do not trade a lot of volume, but are worth keeping an eye on as the liquidity may improve over time. This chapter focuses on the standard VIX futures contracts since that is where the majority of the trading occurs and they are also the main instruments on which the exchange-traded products base their performance.

The nearest expiring VIX future is always the most sensitive to spot VIX changes. If a trader expects a short-term move in spot VIX they should consider the nearest expiring VIX future as the trading instrument that will give them the best exposure to spot VIX price action. In the final chapter, where several volatility events are discussed, I provide an extensive look at how the different available trading products have behaved. Often the near-dated future is the product that would give the best VIX exposure.

To quantitatively determine just how sensitive VIX futures price changes are to the spot VIX index, the beta of VIX futures versus spot VIX based on number of trading days left to expiration was calculated. The results use VIX futures and VIX index daily price changes from 2007 through 2018, and the beta is determined for one through 60 trading days remaining to expiration. Figure 5.3 displays a plot of each average beta by days to expiration using only the standard expiring futures contracts.

Figure 5.3: VIX future price beta relative to spot

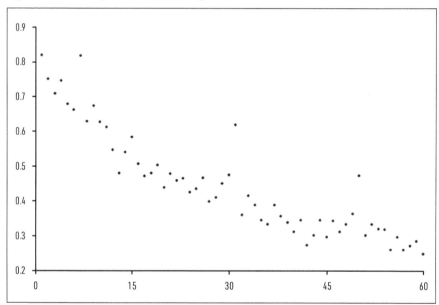

Data source: Bloomberg.

There are a few anomalies, but basically the closer to expiration, the better the VIX futures price tracks spot VIX. On the far right of the chart, the beta falls between 0.25 and 0.30 with 55 to 60 days remaining to expiration. On the far left the beta falls in the 0.70 to 0.80 range with five or fewer days remaining to expiration. As expected, the less time left to expiration, the closer VIX futures price behavior is to that of spot VIX. There are VIX futures expiring each week—however, at the time of publication of this book, the volume has yet to catch on at institutional-size levels. Cboe Global Markets continues to highlight the sensitivity of short-dated VIX futures to spot VIX, so checking to see if the weekly VIX futures volume has increased may be a worthwhile exercise.

VIX FUTURES TERM STRUCTURE

Understanding the relationship between VIX futures pricing and spot VIX is essential when considering trading any of the VIX-related instruments discussed in this book. The term structure of spot VIX and VIX futures was introduced in Chapter 2. Here we take a look at the history behind this pricing relationship.

There are many ways to define the VIX term structure being in either contango or backwardation. Figure 5.4 is a quick refresher of what these two terms look like when charted based on length of time to expiration for each futures contract. Typically, the shape of the curve is a little less smooth than what appears in this generic example. The majority of trading occurs in the first two-month VIX futures contracts.

Figure 5.4: Generic contango/backwardation chart

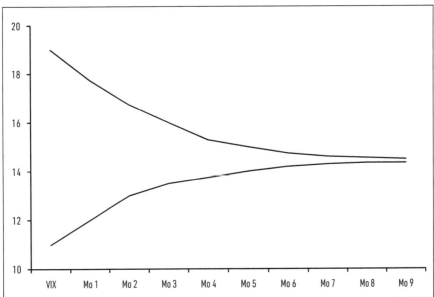

In this chapter the relationship among spot VIX, the first month, and second month futures contracts is used to define when the curve is considered to be in contango or backwardation. There are a couple of reasons for just focusing on the shorter end of the VIX curve. First, the majority of trading occurs in the first two-month VIX futures contracts, so the data can be considered very reliable, even going back to 2007. Also, the largest volatility-related ETPs have positions in only the front two monthly VIX futures contracts, so the relative price of the first and second month VIX futures will influence the performance of these ETPs.

From 2007 to 2019, the VIX index has closed at a discount to the front month VIX futures contract 77.7% of trading days. On 22.2% of trading days VIX was at a premium to the front month future, which leaves three trading days where they were equal.

Table 5.3 breaks out the relationship between the VIX index and the front month futures contract by year. Note that in 2008, spot VIX was at a premium to the front month future just over 45% of trading days. A couple of other years—2007 and 2018—experienced higher than normal price volatility and the result for VIX was spot at a premium to the front month future for a significant number of trading days.

Table 5.3: Relative spot VIX and first month VIX future pricing by year

Year	Trading days	VIX < Mo1	Percent	VIX > Mo1	Percent
2007	251	152	60.56%	99	39.44%
2008	253	138	54.55%	115	45.45%
2009	252	191	75.79%	60	23.81%
2010	252	201	79.76%	51	20.24%
2011	252	180	71.43%	71	28.17%
2012	250	225	90.00%	24	9.60%
2013	252	219	86.90%	33	13.10%
2014	252	209	82.94%	43	17.06%
2015	252	203	80.56%	49	19.44%
2016	252	219	86.90%	33	13.10%
2017	251	242	96.41%	9	3.59%
2018	251	155	61.75%	96	38.25%
2019	252	207	82.14%	45	17.86%

Data source: Bloomberg.

The relationship between the first month and second month futures contracts is similar to that of spot VIX and the front month. On 81% of trading days, the front month future closed lower than the second month contract and 18.3% of the time the front month future closed at a premium to the second month. There are a handful of days where both closed at the same price.

Table 5.4 summarizes a second method of comparing VIX pricing, focusing only on the front two-month VIX futures contracts. These are the two futures that comprise the portfolio that many volatility-related ETPs are charged with holding. The long ETPs benefit when the front month closes at a premium to the second month, while the short ETPs benefit from the negative roll yield associated with the front month trading at a discount to the second month.

Table 5.4: Relative first month and second month VIX futures pricing by year

Year	Trading days	Mo1 < Mo2	Percent	Mo1 > Mo2	Percent
2007	251	177	70.52%	74	29.48%
2008	253	130	51.38%	123	48.62%
2009	252	182	72.22%	68	26.98%
2010	252	235	93.25%	16	6.35%
2011	252	172	68.25%	78	30.95%
2012	250	248	99.20%	2	0.80%
2013	252	242	96.03%	9	3.57%
2014	252	225	89.29%	20	7.94%
2015	252	199	78.97%	52	20.63%
2016	252	216	85.71%	36	14.29%
2017	251	237	94.42%	12	4.78%
2018	251	160	63.75%	88	35.06%
2019	252	226	89.68%	21	8.33%

Data source: Bloomberg.

A final look at the VIX and VIX futures relationship breaks down the number of days where spot VIX is lower than the front month future and the front month future closes at a discount to the second month. This is interpreted as being in contango. The opposite situation, when VIX is higher than the front month and the front month future is higher than the second month is considered backwardation.

Over the 13-year period from 2007 to 2019, the VIX curve was in contango 71.2% of the time. Only 12.3% of observations resulted in backwardation when comparing all three closing prices. There have been a few years where backwardation is priced in by the market well over 90% of days. In fact, in 2012, there was only a single day of contango and this occurred late in the year.

Table 5.5: Spot VIX, first and second month futures pricing relationship by year

Year	Trading days	VIX < Mo1 < Mo2	Percent	VIX > Mo1 > Mo2	Percent
2007	251	132	52.59%	54	21.51%
2008	253	104	41.11%	89	35.18%
2009	252	147	58.33%	25	9.92%
2010	252	201	79.76%	16	6.35%
2011	252	139	55.16%	37	14.68%
2012	250	224	89.60%	1	0.40%
2013	252	218	86.51%	8	3.17%
2014	252	203	80.56%	18	7.14%
2015	252	187	74.21%	36	14.29%
2016	252	205	81.35%	22	8.73%
2017	251	232	92.43%	4	1.59%
2018	251	140	55.78%	75	29.88%
2019	252	199	78.97%	17	6.75%

Data source: Bloomberg.

MODIFIED VIX FUTURE

One attempt at quantifying the relationship between VIX futures and spot VIX is to create a measure that focuses on a consistent time frame. One way to do this is to calculate a consistent 30-day future using a time-weighted average between the first two monthly expirations. The short-dated ETPs focus on this time frame as well, but that index is negatively impacted over time due to a negative roll yield. This modified VIX future which targets the 30-day time frame is just a time-weighted average of two expiring series that is not impacted by any sort of rebalancing cost.

A great benefit of this measure is that it offers a structured method of determining periods of contango and backwardation without the influence of the number of days left to expiration for the futures contracts. When the modified VIX future is at a premium to spot VIX this can be deemed as contango, and when spot VIX closes at a premium to the modified future this could be considered a time where the curve is in backwardation.

Table 5.6: Spot VIX versus modified VIX future by year

Year	Trading days	VIX < future	Percent	VIX > future	Percent
2007	251	177	70.52%	74	29.48%
2008	253	143	56.52%	109	43.08%
2009	252	204	80.95%	47	18.65%
2010	252	219	86.90%	32	12.70%
2011	252	179	71.03%	73	28.97%
2012	250	245	98.00%	5	2.00%
2013	252	232	92.06%	20	7.94%
2014	252	216	85.71%	36	14.29%
2015	252	198	78.57%	54	21.43%
2016	252	223	88.49%	29	11.51%
2017	251	239	95.22%	12	4.78%
2018	251	152	60.56%	99	39.44%
2019	252	224	88.89%	28	11.11%

Data source: Bloomberg.

Table 5.6 shows the modified VIX future price history relative to spot VIX by year. Over the full time period covered in the table, 81% of observations resulted in VIX closing at a discount to the modified VIX future and 18.9% of observations resulted in the consistent 30-day future price closing lower than spot VIX.

WEEKEND IMPACT ON VIX

A final look at VIX price behavior breaks down an anomaly that shows up in spot VIX the day before a weekend. The VIX calculation results in a 30-day forward-looking measure which is specifically calendar days and not trading days. In anticipation of the market being closed for two days, traders will adjust option prices slightly lower as the market close approaches on Friday afternoons. The result of this price adjustment is a slightly lower VIX relative to where it would be trading if the market was not scheduled to be closed for a couple of days.

Table 5.7 breaks down two scenarios that may occur before the weekend. From 2007 to 2019 there have been 594 two-day weekends and 83 three-day weekends. The extra day of the market being closed does impact spot VIX. Note the average daily change for VIX on the Friday before a two-day weekend is a drop of 0.10. On days where the market is going to be closed for three days, the average change for VIX is a drop of 0.26.

Table 5.7: VIX and front two monthly futures performance day before weekend

Two-day weekend				Three-day weekend			
	VIX	Mo 1	Mo 2		VIX	Mo 1	Mo 2
Max.	11.33	6.03	4.50	Max.	3.07	2.90	2.08
Min.	(8.19)	(3.45)	(3.02)	Min.	(4.89)	(3.61)	(1.65)
Average	(0.10)	(0.00)	0.00	Average	(0.26)	(0.06)	(0.02)
% Lower	62.63%	57.58%	53.87%	% Lower	62.65%	51.81%	54.22%

Data source: Bloomberg.

Table 5.7 also displays the impact on VIX futures pricing, focusing on the first month and second month contract. The difference here is negligible, with the front month future losing less than 0.01 before two-day weekends and dropping on average 0.06 before a three-day break. The second month future average change before a two-day weekend is slightly positive, but less than a 0.01. Before a three-day weekend, the second month future loses 0.02 on average. The main takeaway is that this extra day off impacts VIX, but not the tradable VIX futures contract pricing.

The day after a weekend, pricing models are adjusted for the passage of two days and the result is a tailwind for spot VIX. Table 5.8 shows the price behavior for the Monday after a two-day weekend and the first trading day after a three-day weekend. On the Monday after a two-day weekend, VIX will rise an average of 0.27, while on the first trading day after a three-day weekend VIX moves higher by 0.76. The boost after a long weekend is significantly higher than the drop off that occurs before the weekend.

Table 5.8: VIX and front two monthly futures performance day after weekend

Two-day weekend				Three-day weekend			
	VIX	Mo 1	Mo 2		VIX	Mo 1	Mo 2
Max.	20.01	17.60	13.00	Max.	10.54	8.25	6.13
Min.	(17.36)	(10.94)	(3.90)	Min.	(2.90)	(3.40)	(1.65)
Average	0.27	(0.04)	(0.02)	Average	0.76	(0.02)	(0.07)
% Higher	57.4%	40.40%	40.40%	% Higher	59.04%	40.96%	32.53%

Data source: Bloomberg.

In both cases—two-day and three-day weekends—the VIX futures contracts tend to lose a little bit of value. Remember that VIX futures trade at a premium to spot VIX the majority of trading days. VIX futures will lose a little bit of what can be thought of as time value as the contract expiration date approaches. The drop off in pricing on the first day after a weekend is just normal futures behavior.

SUMMARY

- The distribution of VIX closing prices is heavily weighted to lower levels.

- The long-term average closing price for VIX is around 19, but over half the VIX closing prices fall under 17.40.

- The VIX term structure is typically in contango with backwardation occurring during periods of elevated VIX.

- Spot VIX pricing is slightly negatively impacted by days when the market is closed.

71

PART II
TRADES AND STRATEGIES

6

PLANNING A VIX-RELATED TRADE

W HEN I work with a relatively new option trader, they will often inquire about a specific option trade. For instance, asking a question like, "How about I buy the IBM Jan 120 Calls?"

My response to such a question involves stepping back and considering two factors. The first is, "What is the price forecast for shares of the underlying?" In this case IBM. The second is, "What is the timing of that price forecast?"

Using a price forecast and a timing for that outlook, traders may back into the best option trade based on their outlook. VIX trades involve the same sort of process, but several factors may come into play when considering putting on a VIX-related trade.

S&P 500 OUTLOOK

Ultimately, VIX and the associated derivatives instruments have their price activity driven by what is going on in the stock market, specifically with the S&P 500. Typically, VIX gets a lot of attention when the S&P 500 is selling off, even just a couple of percentage points, because the reaction from VIX is normally a quick move to the upside. In fact, the average rally out of VIX from 2007 to 2019, when the S&P 500 is down 2% or more, is a gain of over 17%, with moves well over 20% not uncommon.

The relationship between spot VIX and price changes in the S&P 500 is not fully quantitative. Years ago, Steve Sears from *Barron's* named VIX the "fear index" due to this inverse relationship. However, the truly large upside moves in VIX have occurred when the market is not anticipating what is commonly referred to as a volatility event (trader speak for a stock market sell-off accompanied by a dramatic move higher in VIX).

At a very high level, when a trader has a bearish outlook for the S&P 500, this would lead them to consider a position that would provide long exposure to VIX. Conversely, if a trader believes the S&P 500 is going to move higher, they would get short exposure to VIX. Finally, there are times where the market is rangebound, which can lead to a neutral outlook for the S&P 500. Bullish, bearish, and neutral S&P 500 outlooks all have unique approaches using VIX instruments. In this chapter, a bearish S&P 500 outlook will be used to demonstrate how to trade this type of forecast using VIX-related trading instruments.

BEARISH S&P 500 OUTLOOK

The inverse relationship between VIX and the S&P 500 has already been covered in this book. However, how VIX reacts to a rally or market sell-off is a function of the current level for VIX. If the S&P 500 experiences a 2% sell-off and VIX is at 12, the VIX reaction will be different than if VIX is at 20.

Figure 6.1 shows the high, low, and average VIX one-day change associated with a drop of 2% or more in the S&P 500 from 2007 to 2009. The data is segmented by where the VIX closed the previous day. For example, the far-left bar represents the one-day percentage price change for VIX when the previous day close for VIX was below 15 and the S&P 500 dropped 2% or more on the day.

Figure 6.1: VIX one-day change when S&P 500 is down 2% or more by handle

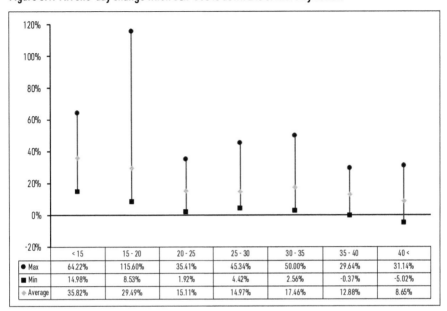

	< 15	15 - 20	20 - 25	25 - 30	30 - 35	35 - 40	40 <
● Max	64.22%	115.60%	35.41%	45.34%	50.00%	29.64%	31.14%
■ Min	14.98%	8.53%	1.92%	4.42%	2.56%	-0.37%	-5.02%
◆ Average	35.82%	29.49%	15.11%	14.97%	17.46%	12.88%	8.65%

Data source: Bloomberg.

Note the average rise for VIX when the S&P 500 drops 2% or more is about 35% when the previous day's close for VIX was 15 or lower. When VIX closed between 15 and 20 the previous day, the average move is under 30%. The average move for VIX moves progressively lower based on the previous day's close being higher. In fact, there are instances of VIX moving lower, despite the S&P 500 dropping 2% or more, when the previous day close for VIX is 35 or higher. VIX indicates how much volatility is anticipated by traders, so when VIX is above 35 it indicates that the market is expecting large moves.

The price action for VIX versus the S&P 500 is interesting, but unfortunately since it is not possible to directly trade the spot VIX index, where the futures are trading relative to the spot index is a big factor when considering a VIX trade. This is not just for a futures trade, but options and ETPs as well, since options and ETPs get their valuation from the futures contracts, not spot VIX.

The more important piece of information is what sort of price change the VIX futures market experienced on the days that the S&P 500 dropped by 2%. The majority of trading is focused on the front month future, especially for short-term trading in the volatility markets. To get a feel for how the active VIX future price changed on the same days, the exercise was repeated substituting the front month future for spot VIX.

Figure 6.2: Active VIX future one-day change when S&P 500 is down 2% or more by handle

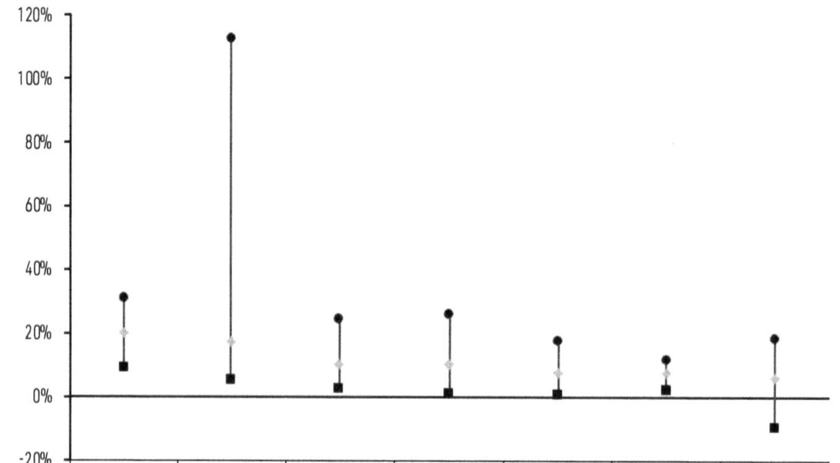

	< 15	15 - 20	20 - 25	25 - 30	30 - 35	35 - 40	40 <
● Max	30.98%	112.64%	24.77%	26.12%	18.03%	11.93%	18.61%
■ Min	9.31%	5.42%	2.91%	1.26%	0.78%	2.16%	-9.34%
◆ Average	20.13%	17.59%	10.10%	10.13%	7.70%	7.66%	6.11%

Data source: Bloomberg.

The price reaction from the front month VIX futures contract mirrors the direction of moves for spot VIX, but not the magnitude of those moves. Figure 6.3 shows the relative price move, broken down by spot VIX price handles.

Figure 6.3: Relative VIX future and spot VIX price change when S&P 500 is down 2% or more by handle

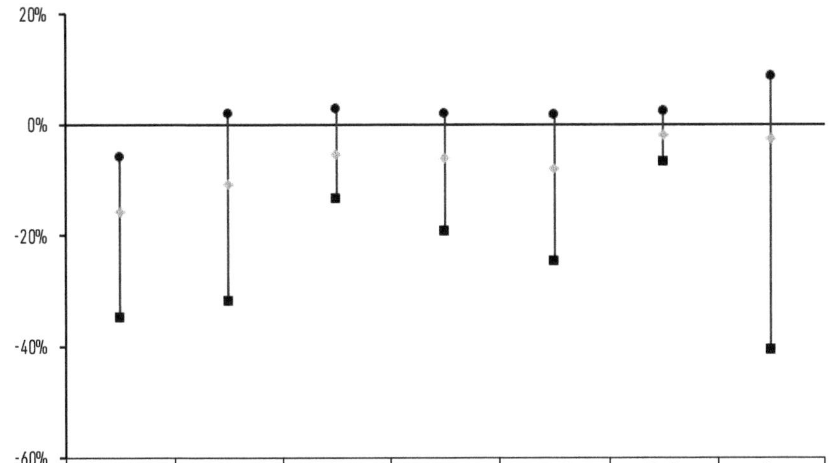

	< 15	15 - 20	20 - 25	25 - 30	30 - 35	35 - 40	40 <
● Max	-5.67%	2.02%	2.95%	2.04%	1.81%	2.53%	8.80%
■ Min	-34.76%	-31.58%	-13.36%	-19.09%	-24.61%	-6.69%	-40.48%
◆ Average	-15.69%	-10.64%	-5.31%	-6.04%	-7.87%	-1.95%	-2.44%

Data source: Bloomberg.

Note that on average when VIX closed the day before at 15 or lower and the S&P 500 sells off 2%, the front month futures underperform spot VIX by about 15%. The higher the VIX price, the less the percentage underperformance. Also note that the VIX price changes are not as dramatic when VIX is over 40 as they are when VIX is under 15.

The point behind this exercise is that when planning a VIX trade, the first step is to look to where the future is trading relative to spot VIX. If spot VIX is at 20.00 and with three days until expiration the front month futures contract is trading at 25.00, it does not make much sense to purchase the VIX future or pursue any other long trade that has pricing based on this futures contract. Many traders that are new to VIX are often disappointed when they catch a volatility spike, but the future or other instrument they chose to express this outlook does not pay off as much as they expected. This is a reality of trading VIX futures, options, and ETPs.

VIX INDEX PRICING

The spot VIX index historically has been as low as 9 and as high as the 80s. VIX goes through periods where what is defined as 'high' or 'low' is relative. For instance, in 2009 the S&P 500 rallied by about 50% from March through the end of the year. Over that massive bullish run, VIX remained above 20. In fact, breaking the 20 level was thought to be a low level. Fast forward to the past few years where VIX has languished in the 10 to 12 range.

VIX FUTURE PRICING

Ultimately, any instrument used to trade an outlook for VIX wins or loses based on the price behavior of VIX futures contracts. A VIX futures price is based on a forward value of VIX and this forward value of VIX may be thought of as having two components. The two factors are a risk premium that entices market participants to consider taking a short position in the future, and potentially a market opinion as to where spot VIX will trade at expiration.

When VIX is low and the stock market has not been experiencing much price volatility, there is a risk premium in the VIX futures price that is compensating traders for selling that contract. As noted in Chapters 2 and 5, when VIX spikes up, the VIX curve will move into backwardation where spot VIX is at a premium to the futures contract. The underperformance of VIX futures noted in this chapter is the result of this sort of price action. When the VIX index is higher than VIX futures pricing, the expected direction for spot VIX takes over as the major influence on VIX futures pricing. Traders are aware that most VIX spikes are short-lived and based on that typical price action they do not bid up VIX futures prices when the spot VIX index moves up quickly.

When considering a VIX-related trade, the VIX futures contracts that correspond to the outlook being traded will often be a dominant factor in planning the trade. Specific points to keep in mind are where is the future relative to spot VIX, and how much time is left until the futures contract expires?

Consider the price action for VIX and the front month future over a short period of time, as shown in Figure 6.4. This is the case where spot VIX moved up quickly and a short position in the front month future would have resulted in a loss, even though the index was lower a few days later.

Figure 6.4: Daily prices for VIX index and December VIX future (December 4–December 13, 2018)

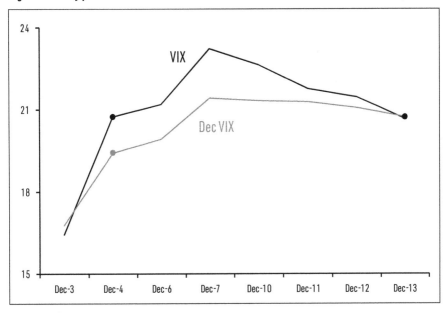

Data source: Bloomberg.

On December 4, VIX closed at 20.74, up 26.2% on the day, while the December VIX future moved higher, settling at 19.425, up 15.8% on the day. Both these data points are highlighted on the chart. Over the course of a few days, VIX moved up and then closed slightly lower on December 13. Over the same time frame, the December contract drifted higher, but on December 13 the settlement price was 20.725, 1.30 higher than the December 4 close.

The volatility-related ETP price behavior is tied to VIX futures. The short-term ETPs specifically are impacted by the price behavior of the front two-month futures contracts. Figure 6.5 covers the same time period as the previous chart, but instead of the front month futures contract, the daily price changes for VXX focused on shorter-dated futures are demonstrated.

Figure 6.5: Daily prices for VIX index and VXX (December 4–December 13, 2018)

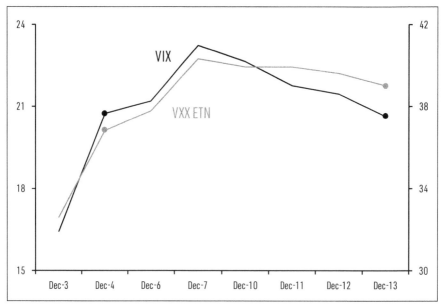

Data source: Bloomberg.

Once again, VIX was down slightly from the December 4 close to the December 13 close. Over the same time period, VXX rose from 36.84 to 39.01, a gain of 5.9%. Both a short position in the futures or VXX resulted in a loss, despite a drop in VIX.

This example highlights how important it is to compare VIX futures prices to that of spot VIX when considering any VIX-related trade, whether long or short, as ultimately the outcome of the trade will rely on VIX futures price action and not spot VIX.

The next three chapters discuss different approaches to trading volatility-linked futures, options, and ETPs based on three general outlooks.

Systematically short trading both VIX and VSTOXX futures is covered in Chapter 7. In Chapter 8, shorting volatility spikes is covered. In Chapter 9 some approaches to having long volatility exposure, a trade that is wrong more often than right, is discussed. Finally, Chapter 10 discusses spread trading VIX futures against each other as a calendar spread along with combining VIX and VSTOXX futures into a single spread position.

SUMMARY

- An outlook for the S&P 500, VIX, and VIX futures pricing all come into play when planning a VIX-related trade.

- Not only should there be a directional outlook for the S&P 500, but also an opinion as to how the price action will play out.

- A long VIX strategy is best implemented when a large unexpected drop in the S&P 500 is forecast.

- VIX futures price relative to spot VIX will influence what strategy is considered based on a trader's outlook for VIX.

7
SYSTEMATICALLY SHORTING VOLATILITY

MOST OF the attention that VIX gets occurs on days where the stock market is down and VIX is spiking to high levels. However, a large number of traders have become attracted to VIX trading instruments in order to take advantage of some common pricing characteristics of VIX. Specifically, VIX futures often trade at a premium to spot VIX and the price converges with spot VIX as expiration approaches.

A short VIX position can be initiated with futures, options, or ETPs. The core price behavior of options and ETPs relates to the futures contracts and this chapter focuses on the behavior of VIX futures in what would be considered fairly normal volatility environments. Chapter 8 explores initiating short positions when VIX experiences a quick move to the upside, which is a very different method of getting short exposure to VIX.

CBOE INDEXES

Cboe is a leader in creating strategy-based indexes and there are two that demonstrate the performance of a consistent short position in VIX futures contracts. The Cboe VIX Premium Strategy Index (VPD^{SM}) and Cboe

Capped VIX Premium Strategy Index (VPN^SM) have slightly different structures, but are good resources to get a feel for how a consistent strategy shorting VIX futures contracts performs.

The strategy behind VPD involves consistently selling front month VIX futures combined with a money market account. The number of VIX futures sold on each roll date is determined through assuming that a 25-point move to the upside in the contract would result in the portfolio losing 25%. The index has been calculated from late 2004. However, since VIX futures trading really did not reach sufficient volumes to implement strategies until late 2006, the performance in Figure 7.1 starts on the last day of 2006.

Figure 7.1: Cboe VIX Premium Strategy Index performance (2007–2019)

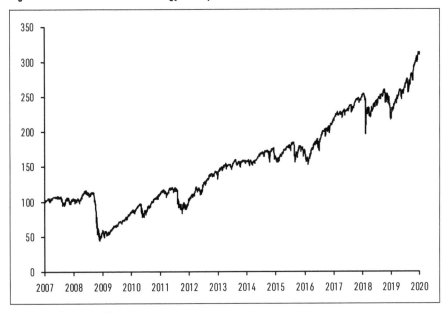

Data source: Cboe Global Markets.

A portfolio of $100 following the strategy VPD measures would have grown to about $313 over the 13-year period covered in the chart. Do note there are some extreme drawdowns by blindly following this strategy. For example, during the Great Financial Crisis this strategy lost over 50% in a short period of time.

The Cboe Capped VIX Premium Strategy Index, or VPN, also maintains a short position in VIX futures. However, instead of selling VIX futures based on a potential 25% drawdown, this strategy purchases call options to hedge against a move to the upside. The specific options purchased are the closest strike at or below 25 points higher than the VIX futures price. The multiplier for VIX options is 100 and for VIX futures it is 1000, therefore this strategy will buy 10 VIX call options for each short VIX future. Figure 7.2 shows the performance of this strategy over the 13-year period from 2007 to 2019.

Figure 7.2: Cboe Capped VIX Premium Strategy Index performance (2007–2019)

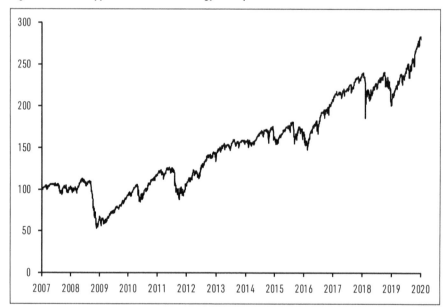

Data source: Cboe Global Markets.

The shape of the VPN chart is very similar to that of VPD, but underperforms VPD, with $100 invested in VPN growing to about $283 at the end of 2019. The cost of hedging the short VIX futures has a slight negative impact on performance, but also results in drawdowns not being as dramatic.

Both VPD and VPN are profitable over a long period of time. However, both also experience very dramatic drawdowns. These drawdowns make blindly following each of these strategies unpalatable for most traders and investors. However, the indexes are useful as they demonstrate how short volatility works over a long period of time, as well as how treacherous this approach can be with respect to periodic drawdowns.

ABOUT VIX EXPIRATION

All the details regarding how the final settlement price for VIX futures and options is determined may be found at www.cboe.com. This book focuses on price behavior, trading strategies, and some history around VIX, and leaves the mundane details to the good folks at Cboe Global Markets. However, with respect to this chapter, understanding some of the details is important.

VIX futures and options are typically settled on a Wednesday. Before non-standard weekly expirations were available for trading, this was always the Wednesday that was 30 days before the third Friday of the following month. Settlement is calculated using relevant SPX opening option prices on settlement Wednesday. AM settlement for any derivative contract has the unique issue of overnight risk along with risk that opening prices are skewed in one direction or another. At times, this has shown up in VIX, with settlement being much higher or much lower than the previous day's close. Because of this, the systematic approach to trading VIX futures introduced in this chapter encourages traders to exit their position the day before VIX settlement, typically a Tuesday.

VIX FUTURES PRICE BEHAVIOR INTO EXPIRATION

The price relationship between spot VIX and VIX futures based on the number of trading days remaining until expiration was covered in Chapter 5. The closer the contract is to expiration, the higher the beta of VIX futures daily price changes relative to spot VIX. This is a function of VIX futures prices gravitating to the level of spot VIX since VIX futures settle into a calculation of VIX.

Another aspect of VIX futures relative to spot VIX is that VIX futures are priced at a premium to spot VIX more often than not. This shows up in the shape of the VIX term structure, which is usually in contango as the price of the futures increases relative to spot VIX the longer to expiration.

The method of trading VIX futures into expiration discussed in this chapter combines these two known pieces of VIX price behavior: VIX futures usually trade at a premium to spot VIX and VIX futures prices gravitate to spot VIX as expiration approaches. Quantitative or systematic approaches need to have both logic and a result that has worked historically. This approach has both.

VIX INDEX AND FUTURES DATA

The data used for this testing combines spot VIX index closing figures gathered from Yahoo Finance, along with daily VIX futures settlement prices downloaded and formatted for testing from www.cfe.cboe.com. Cboe Global Markets shares VIX futures data going back to inception.

A final note about the data: early on, VIX futures prices were 10x that of the spot index, so if VIX is at 15 the comparable futures price would be 150. Some early VIX futures prices were adjusted by dividing the settlement by 10 to make the figures match the current price convention.

TABLE EXPLANATIONS

Each table shows the price change for VIX futures from a certain number of days to expiration through the settlement price the day before expiration. Here are some descriptions for the various columns on the tables in this chapter:

- **Days to expiration**—the number of trading days until expiration.

- **Total points**—the sum of all observed price changes. Negative numbers indicate a short position would be profitable.

- **Observations**—how many price changes that were recorded. A filter will be applied so the number of observations will change based on filtering.

- **VIX future lower**—the number of observations where the VIX future price change was lower between the settlement on the days to expiration and the settlement the day before expiration.

- **% VIX future lower**—percent of observations where prices were lower the day before expiration versus the respective days left to expiration.

- **Maximum down move**—largest observed price drop over single observation.

- **Maximum up move**—largest observed price rise over single observation.

- **Average move**—average price change for all observations.

TEST 1: STANDARD FUTURES BEFORE VIX WEEKLYS

VIX Weeklys futures contracts were introduced in late July 2015. Because the introduction of new expirations may have an impact on the use of standard contracts, a test was run to explore the behavior of futures into expiration covering the January 2007 through July 2015 standard VIX future contracts.

This involves 103 observations and the first test explores how VIX futures pricing behaved over the last nine days before expiration through the settlement the night before expiration. Table 7.1 shows the results of this testing.

Table 7.1: Price action of standard VIX futures leading up to expiration (January 2007–July 2015)

Days to expiration	Total points	Observations	VIX future lower	% VIX future lower	Maximum down move	Maximum up move	Average move
9	-77.75	103	68	66.02%	-8.05	14.38	-0.75
8	-68.50	103	69	66.99%	-7.70	14.93	-0.67
7	-49.93	103	66	64.08%	-9.60	13.35	-0.48
6	-42.63	103	68	66.02%	-7.60	9.86	-0.41
5	-71.73	103	73	70.87%	-7.60	11.23	-0.70
4	-42.49	103	69	66.99%	-11.08	10.17	-0.41
3	-45.47	103	68	66.02%	-10.45	5.45	-0.44
2	-23.16	103	65	63.11%	-5.19	8.25	-0.22

Between 63.11% and 70.87% of observations across all days to expiration the VIX future price moved lower between the daily settlement price and the settlement the night before Wednesday AM expiration. The average price changes varied from a low of –0.22 between two days to expiration and the day before expiration, and –0.75 when taking the closing price nine days before expiration and comparing this to the closing future price the day before expiration.

Shorting volatility without any sort of hedge is a very risky approach to trading. The column that indicates the **Maximum up move** shows the worst-case scenario over the observations for a short trade. There are some very large numbers in this column, with several instances of a move of over 10 points to the upside over these short periods of time.

Remember the concept behind this methodology is based on VIX futures usually trading at a premium to spot VIX. The first study does not take this into account, as it just automatically sells VIX futures.

The second study removes any occurrence where a VIX futures settlement price is lower than that of spot VIX. This system involves being short VIX futures and so it is logical to focus on just the instances where the futures settle at a premium to the spot index to align with this approach. Anywhere from 22 to 41 observations were removed in this part of the study, depending on the time to expiration due to the future price closing at a discount to spot VIX on the entry day.

The result of removing instances where VIX futures were lower than spot VIX results in some improvement in the percentage of observations where the futures prices are lower on the settlement the day before expiration. Those results appear in Table 7.2.

Table 7.2: Filtered price action of monthly VIX futures leading up to expiration (January 2007–July 2015)

Days to expiration	Total points	Observations	VIX future lower	% VIX future lower	Maximum down move	Maximum up move	Average move
9	−64.03	72	52	72.22%	−7.00	14.38	−0.89
8	−32.98	81	51	62.96%	−5.80	14.93	−0.41
7	−22.11	77	47	61.04%	−6.10	13.35	−0.29
6	−37.91	77	51	66.23%	−5.00	9.86	−0.49
5	−40.85	73	51	69.86%	−6.50	11.23	−0.56
4	−42.78	77	56	72.73%	−4.80	6.11	−0.56
3	−32.30	81	55	67.90%	−4.83	5.45	−0.40
2	−3.40	62	41	66.13%	−2.40	8.25	−0.05

There are fewer trading opportunities based on using this filter, but over much of the time period there is a slight improvement in the percentage of observations where the future price is lower over the time period observed. The average move over the various time periods changes in both directions, with a very dramatic change in the two-day time period. A good portion of the observations were eliminated, but the biggest **Maximum up move** was not avoided. One time period that stands out is four days to expiration which, with VIX settlement on Wednesday AM, would be the Thursday the week before. Note the average move is 0.15 better using the filter and the **Maximum up move** of 10.17 drops to 6.11. The **Percent future lower** statistic also improves by about 5%.

TEST 2: ALL EXPIRATIONS AFTER THE INTRODUCTION OF WEEKLYS

As noted, VIX futures that expire every week were introduced in late July 2015. The next step in exploring how VIX futures behave as expiration approaches takes a look at all futures contracts, standard and weekly, from August 2015 through the end of 2019.

Table 7.3 shows the price behavior for all contracts over this time period, which covers 233 observations including all standard and weekly VIX futures contracts from August 2015 through December 2019. The average move is lower than what was noted in Table 7.1. The percentage of observations that result in the VIX future price lower on the day before expiration versus where it was when a short trade would be initiated is mostly lower than previous results. Also, there are some instances of a large move higher that are much greater than the first non-filtered test results.

Table 7.3: Price action of all VIX futures leading up to expiration (August 2015–December 2019)

Days to expiration	Total points	Observations	VIX future lower	% VIX future lower	Maximum down move	Maximum up move	Average move
9	−81.33	233	162	69.53%	−6.58	21.18	−0.35
8	−62.93	233	159	68.24%	−6.65	21.13	−0.27
7	−80.28	233	153	65.67%	−8.00	21.40	−0.34
6	−55.05	233	153	65.67%	−7.35	21.15	−0.24
5	−41.90	233	154	66.09%	−5.80	20.30	−0.18
4	−33.78	233	150	64.38%	−4.55	17.28	−0.14
3	−22.85	233	143	61.37%	−4.70	12.45	−0.10
2	−17.20	233	132	56.65%	−5.73	6.63	−0.07

Using a filter of only shorting the VIX future when it closes higher than spot VIX is shown in Table 7.4. The win percentage is a bit lower than the unfiltered results in the previous table. A dramatic improvement in the **Maximum up move** column for instances with four or fewer days remaining stands out on these filtered results.

Table 7.4: Filtered price action of all VIX futures leading up to expiration (August 2015–December 2019)

Days to expiration	Total points	Observations	VIX future lower	% VIX future lower	Maximum down move	Maximum up move	Average move
9	−54.50	184	128	69.57%	−4.70	21.18	−0.30
8	−36.68	193	134	69.43%	−4.00	21.13	−0.19
7	−25.75	182	121	66.48%	−5.45	21.40	−0.14
6	−48.00	177	119	67.23%	−7.05	21.15	−0.27
5	−37.65	176	118	67.05%	−5.25	20.30	−0.21
4	−46.53	187	122	65.24%	−4.00	5.10	−0.25
3	−31.10	199	124	62.31%	−2.95	6.15	−0.16
2	−2.35	173	92	53.18%	−3.43	3.13	−0.01

TEST 3: ONLY VIX WEEKLY FUTURES

As of late 2019, Weekly VIX futures liquidity is not consistent enough for institutions to consider trading in a systematic manner. With this in mind, the price behavior using only the Weekly contracts is broken out into a single study which is followed by observing only the standard VIX futures contracts over the time period since the weekly contracts have become available (see Test 4).

Table 7.5 highlights how Weekly VIX futures prices have behaved since introduction through the end of 2019 over the final few days through settlement. The statistics are similar to the results in Table 7.3 which is a function of the observations in Table 7.5 making up a majority of the observations in Table 7.3.

Table 7.5: Price action of Weekly VIX futures leading up to expiration
(August 2015–December 2019)

Days to expiration	Total points	Observations	VIX future lower	% VIX future lower	Maximum down move	Maximum up move	Average move
9	−55.05	180	127	70.56%	−6.33	21.18	−0.31
8	−39.45	180	123	68.33%	−6.65	21.13	−0.22
7	−34.40	180	119	66.11%	−8.00	21.40	−0.19
6	−22.63	180	115	63.89%	−7.35	21.15	−0.13
5	−4.08	180	114	63.33%	−5.80	20.30	−0.02
4	0.23	180	112	62.22%	−4.55	17.28	0.00
3	−2.33	180	106	58.89%	−4.70	12.45	−0.01
2	−8.60	180	104	57.78%	−5.73	6.63	−0.05

The price action when only recording observations when the futures contract is higher than spot VIX appear in Table 7.6. This is an interesting set of results, which opens up questions as to the shorter-dated VIX futures price action.

Table 7.6: Filtered price action of Weekly VIX futures leading up to expiration
(August 2015–December 2018)

Days to expiration	Total points	Observations	VIX future lower	% VIX future lower	Maximum down move	Maximum up move	Average move
9	−29.83	139	98	70.50%	−4.70	21.18	−0.21
8	−10.05	146	101	69.18%	−3.65	21.13	−0.07
7	1.13	139	93	66.91%	−3.48	21.40	0.01
6	−27.23	135	88	65.19%	−7.05	21.15	−0.20
5	−10.30	135	85	62.96%	−5.25	20.30	−0.08
4	−23.83	144	91	63.19%	−3.33	4.93	−0.17
3	−22.98	154	94	61.04%	−2.95	6.15	−0.15
2	0.75	135	74	54.81%	−3.43	3.13	0.01

Note that with the VIX Weeklys, the filtered results are somewhat erratic. A consistent trade with two days to expiration that is exited the following day would actually be a losing approach, as would the same with seven days to expiration. The three- and four-day results are slightly better, but the win percentage for each of these is around 60%. It may be that avoiding this sort of trade with the non-standard VIX futures is a good idea, not just because of a lack of liquidity.

TEST 4: ONLY STANDARD VIX FUTURES (AUGUST 2015–DECEMBER 2019)

The standard VIX futures contract price activity, since the introduction of the short-dated contracts, is covered in Tables 7.7 and 7.8. Table 7.7 covers the non-filtered results over 53 months.

Table 7.7: Price action of all standard VIX futures leading up to expiration (August 2015–December 2019)

Days to expiration	Total points	Observations	VIX future lower	% VIX future lower	Maximum down move	Maximum up move	Average move
9	−26.28	53	35	66.04%	−6.58	11.95	−0.50
8	−23.48	53	36	67.92%	−6.13	9.60	−0.44
7	−45.88	53	34	64.15%	−8.00	6.10	−0.87
6	−32.43	53	38	71.70%	−6.45	5.85	−0.61
5	−37.83	53	40	75.47%	−4.95	5.60	−0.71
4	−34.00	53	38	71.70%	−4.00	5.10	−0.64
3	−20.53	53	37	69.81%	−3.40	3.90	−0.39
2	−8.60	53	28	52.83%	−2.45	2.25	−0.16

The **% VIX future lower** statistic is very similar to the figures in Table 7.1 which show standard VIX futures results prior to the introduction of the non-standard VIX futures contracts. These figures greatly contrast with the results in Table 7.5 which covers the unfiltered results for the Weekly VIX futures.

Table 7.8 filters out any instances where the VIX future closed lower than the spot VIX index. The two-day result falls below 50% and the average profit for the three days until expiration trade witnesses a drop in the total points gained through a systematic approach.

Table 7.8: Filtered price action of all standard VIX futures leading up to expiration (August 2015–December 2019)

Days to expiration	Total points	Observations	VIX future lower	% VIX future lower	Maximum down move	Maximum up move	Average move
9	−24.68	45	30	66.67%	−4.03	5.75	−0.55
8	−26.63	47	33	70.21%	−4.00	5.85	−0.57
7	−26.88	43	28	65.12%	−5.45	6.10	−0.63
6	−20.78	42	31	73.81%	−3.10	5.85	−0.49
5	−27.35	41	33	80.49%	−2.50	5.60	−0.67
4	−22.70	43	31	72.09%	−4.00	5.10	−0.53
3	−8.12	45	30	66.67%	−2.60	3.90	−0.18
2	−3.10	38	18	47.37%	−2.15	1.50	−0.08

The results for the Weekly futures fall short of the results for the standard futures since the introduction of the Weeklys. It may be a lack of liquidity or some other factor coming into play here. It is not that shorting volatility when the futures are at a premium to VIX using the Weekly VIX futures or associated instruments is a losing proposition, it just appears that it is not as consistent as doing so only with the established standard VIX futures.

TEST 5: ONLY STANDARD VIX FUTURES (JANUARY 2007–DECEMBER 2019)

A final look at how VIX futures behave as expiration approaches appears in Table 7.9 and 7.10. The first table shows the results using VIX futures with no screen through the close before settlement. The statistics are in line with the other results that show VIX futures generally drift lower as expiration approaches.

Table 7.9: Price action of all standard VIX futures leading up to expiration (January 2007–December 2019)

Days to expiration	Total points	Observations	VIX future lower	% VIX future lower	Maximum down move	Maximum up move	Average move
9	-104.03	156	103	66.03%	-8.05	14.38	-0.67
8	-91.97	156	105	67.31%	-7.70	14.93	-0.59
7	-95.80	156	100	64.10%	-9.60	13.35	-0.61
6	-75.05	156	106	67.95%	-7.60	9.86	-0.48
5	-109.55	156	113	72.44%	-7.60	11.23	-0.70
4	-76.49	156	107	68.59%	-11.08	10.17	-0.42
3	-66.00	156	105	67.31%	-10.45	5.45	-0.46
2	-31.76	156	93	59.62%	-5.19	8.25	-0.20

Table 7.10 shows the filtered results when filtering out instances of the VIX futures closing lower than spot VIX. These figures form the basis for what can be a systematic approach to short volatility in the right market conditions. One thing to note about the maximum up moves on this table is that they all occurred before VIX Weeklys were introduced.

Table 7.10: Filtered price action of standard VIX futures leading up to expiration (January 2007–December 2019)

Days to expiration	Total points	Observations	VIX future lower	% VIX future lower	Maximum down move	Maximum up move	Average move
9	-88.70	117	82	70.09%	-7.00	14.38	-0.76
8	-59.60	128	84	65.63%	-5.80	14.93	-0.47
7	-48.98	120	75	62.50%	-6.10	13.35	-0.41
6	-58.68	119	82	68.91%	-5.00	9.86	-0.49
5	-68.20	114	84	73.68%	-6.50	11.23	-0.60
4	-65.48	120	87	72.50%	-4.80	6.11	-0.55
3	-40.43	126	85	67.46%	-4.83	5.45	-0.32
2	-6.50	100	59	59.00%	-2.40	8.25	-0.07

There are many methods that can be implemented using the statistical information that shows the behavior of VIX futures. A straightforward one is selling the front month future. A calendar spread, selling the near month and buying a later month, can make sense as well. Also, since VIX options share a forward pricing outlook with the futures contract that shares an expiration, selling a call option to take advantage of time decay along with price decay, or purchasing a deep-in-the-money put option with very little time value, are both viable alternatives to directly trading futures.

Also, entry and exit rules are very basic for the tables above. A buffer of more than just having the futures at a premium to spot VIX may reduce the number of trades, but improve the results. An exit strategy that includes a stop if the curve inverts, as opposed to holding the trade through the day before expiration, can improve results as well.

VSTOXX FUTURES

VSTOXX futures contracts exhibit the same sort of price behavior as VIX futures contracts. The same testing applied to VIX futures was used to highlight how VSTOXX futures behave as expiration approaches. Table 7.11 shows the price behavior for VSTOXX contracts from two to nine days before the contract expires through the closing price the day before expiration.

Table 7.11: Price action of standard VSTOXX futures leading up to expiration
(January 2010–December 2019)

Days to expiration	Total points	Observations	VSTOXX future lower	% VSTOXX future lower	Maximum down move	Maximum up move	Average move
9	-65.35	120	77	64.17%	-7.85	12.75	-0.54
8	-67.80	120	82	68.33%	-7.90	12.25	-0.57
7	-71.60	120	83	69.17%	-9.30	12.50	-0.60
6	-65.60	120	78	65.00%	-10.30	13.05	-0.55
5	-63.80	120	80	66.67%	-7.50	12.15	-0.53
4	-60.05	120	87	72.50%	-5.80	10.90	-0.50
3	-57.00	120	82	68.33%	-5.85	7.55	-0.48
2	-40.40	120	76	63.33%	-3.60	4.70	-0.34

The unfiltered results cover 10 years or 120 observations. The figures actually look very similar to the 13 years of history shown for VIX futures. The win percentage ranges from 63.33% to 72.50%, and the average move ranges from −0.34 to −0.60. One difference is the **Maximum up moves** are mostly higher, but not to a significantly different level to that of VIX.

Table 7.12 filters out instances where the futures are at a discount to the spot VSTOXX index.

Table 7.12: Filtered price action of standard VSTOXX futures leading up to expiration (January 2010–December 2019)

Days to expiration	Total points	Observations	VSTOXX future lower	% VSTOXX future lower	Maximum down move	Maximum up move	Average move
9	−57.80	75	51	68.00%	−5.40	12.75	−0.77
8	−59.70	79	58	73.42%	−4.50	12.25	−0.76
7	−32.60	70	49	70.00%	−4.70	12.50	−0.47
6	−34.60	68	46	67.65%	−5.25	13.05	−0.51
5	−22.00	63	43	68.25%	−3.35	12.15	−0.35
4	−42.15	76	60	78.95%	−5.80	10.90	−0.55
3	−19.30	81	55	67.90%	−3.70	7.55	−0.24
2	−23.35	68	43	63.24%	−2.30	3.10	−0.34

Using a filter to avoid instances where the futures close lower than the index improves the win percentage as well as the average trade result for several of the time periods covered in this study. Like VIX, there are also VSTOXX option contracts that offer alternative approaches to systematically trading to take advantage of futures drifting lower, towards parity with the index, as expiration approaches.

SUMMARY

- VIX futures pricing will gravitate toward spot VIX as expiration approaches.

- Consistently shorting VIX futures when they are at a premium to spot VIX is an effective method of shorting volatility.

- The introduction of VIX Weeklys did not have an impact on the price behavior of monthly VIX futures.

- VSTOXX futures offer the same opportunity to short volatility as expiration approaches.

8
SHORTING VOLATILITY SPIKES

VIX RECEIVED the moniker "fear index" due to its price behavior when the stock market experiences a quick and dramatic sell-off. What does not get as much attention, because it is not quite as exciting, is the behavior of VIX after one of these dramatic sell-offs.

VIX SPIKES

Volatility expectations as determined by option pricing vary from market to market. The one characteristic that is common is that volatility is a mean reverting measure. Figure 8.1 shows daily VIX price action in 2018, which was a year that gave us a few quick upside moves.

Figure 8.1: Daily VIX versus 20-day moving average (2018)

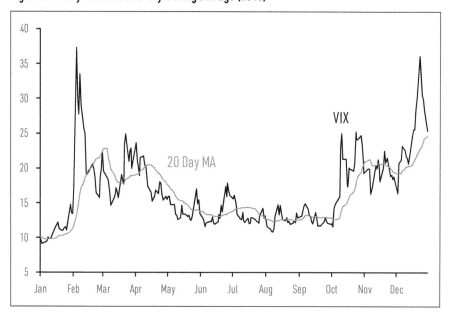

Data source: Bloomberg.

The dark line in Figure 8.1 represents the daily closing price for VIX, while the lighter line is the 20-day moving average for VIX. Note that each of the VIX spikes was followed by a move back to this moving average. The final quick move to the upside out of VIX occurred very close to the end of the year. Less than a week after the start of 2019, VIX was back under this moving average once again.

There is nothing magical about the 20-day moving average. It is just my preference for a short-term indicator. Looking at the data from 2007 through the end of 2019, VIX closed under this moving average about 59% of trading days and spent the other 41% above this average. This may be interpreted as VIX spending more time below than above the 20-day moving average.

A very high-level test looks at how long it takes VIX to retrace half of a 25% or greater one-day move to the upside. From 2007 to 2019, there have been 41 one-day moves greater than 25% to the upside. Five of those occurred during a period when VIX had not retraced half of the 25% move, so there is a little overlap in the data. Those observations occurred in August 2011, August 2015, and February 2018, which are all volatility events that are discussed in the final chapter of this book. These three instances are worth remembering, as selling volatility after the first 25% move up would have resulted in experiencing at least one more volatility spike after entering some sort of short trade. Table 8.1 summarizes the price action of VIX after a one-day 25% move to the upside.

Table 8.1: Summary of price action after a 25% one-day upside move for VIX

Spike date	Size of move	Days to 50% retrace	Spike date	Size of move	Days to 50% retrace
2/27/2007	64.22%	7	8/20/2015	25.51%	35
3/13/2007	29.59%	4	8/21/2015	46.45%	14
11/1/2007	25.26%	25	8/24/2015	45.34%	2
6/6/2008	26.46%	6	12/11/2015	26.11%	2
9/29/2008	34.48%	1	6/24/2016	49.33%	2
10/15/2008	25.61%	3	9/9/2016	39.89%	8
10/22/2008	31.14%	7	5/17/2017	46.38%	2
4/27/2010	30.57%	2	8/10/2017	44.37%	2
5/6/2010	31.67%	2	8/17/2017	32.45%	2
5/20/2010	29.64%	1	2/2/2018	28.51%	24
2/22/2011	26.60%	4	2/5/2018	115.60%	5
8/4/2011	35.41%	59	3/22/2018	30.68%	5
8/8/2011	50.00%	1	5/29/2018	28.74%	1
8/18/2011	35.12%	3	6/25/2018	25.85%	7
11/9/2011	31.59%	2	10/10/2018	43.95%	4
2/25/2013	34.02%	2	12/4/2018	26.16%	25
4/15/2013	43.20%	1	5/7/2019	25.13%	3
1/24/2014	31.74%	2	5/13/2019	28.12%	1
7/17/2014	32.18%	1	8/5/2019	39.64%	1
7/31/2014	27.16%	2	8/14/2019	26.14%	2
6/29/2015	34.45%	2			

Data source: Bloomberg.

On average it takes VIX about seven trading days to retrace half of a greater than 25% one-day move. This is defined as moving lower by at least 50% of the point move on the day VIX rallied. Of the 41 observations, VIX retraced this level within five trading days 30 times, and retraced half the rally 35 times within a 10-trading-day period.

There are some major outliers. For instance, on August 4, 2011 VIX rallied by 35% from 23.38 to 31.66. A 50% retracement of this move, closing below 27.52, was not established until October 27, 2011 when VIX closed at 25.46. That is 59 trading days. The few instances where it took more than 20 days for VIX to retrace half of a spike to the upside appear in Table 8.2.

Table 8.2: Summary of instances where 50% retracement took more than 20 days

Spike date	Close	1 Day % change	Retrace date	Close	Trading days	Second spike?
11/1/2007	23.21	25.26%	12/7/2007	20.85	25	No
8/4/2011	31.66	35.41%	10/27/2011	25.46	59	Yes
8/20/2015	19.14	25.51%	10/9/2015	17.08	35	Yes
2/2/2018	17.31	28.51%	3/9/2018	14.64	24	Yes
12/4/2018	20.74	26.16%	1/11/2019	18.19	25	No

Data source: Bloomberg.

There is no pattern to these instances where VIX remained at high levels for several weeks. The one-day price changes are actually on the low end of the range of 25% or greater VIX index price moves. One piece of information to definitely remember is that of these five protracted time periods that VIX remained high, three also resulted in a second 25% plus move to the upside.

These statistics on spot VIX are very interesting, but more important for trading purposes is the behavior of the VIX futures markets during periods where VIX rallied quickly in a single day. A major issue with shorting VIX futures after a spike in VIX is that the VIX term structure curve usually moves into backwardation when there is a spike in the spot VIX index. Volatility traders are aware that VIX tends to spike and then move lower, based on this fairly consistent price action, and so traders are not going to bid the price of VIX futures up when there is time remaining until final settlement.

Shorting the futures and then covering when half the index move to the upside was retraced would result in fairly decent long-term returns.

To test this, a short position in the front month future and then covering that short upon a 50% index retracement was replicated. There were a few instances where the short future position would need to be rolled to the following month.

In one particular case, August to October 2011, the short position would need to be rolled three times. The result using futures in this manner is an average profit of just over 1 point a trade.

There were several instances where shorting the futures contract and holding until the index had retraced 50% of the spike was a losing trade.

Table 8.3 is a high-level review of how just shorting VIX futures and holding until the index retraced half of the move would have worked.

Table 8.3: Summary of shorting VIX futures when spot VIX spikes 25%

Trades	Winners	Win %	Total profit	Average trade
41	33	80.49%	43.82	1.07

Worst drawdown	Best drawdown	Average drawdown
−17.60	6.05	−1.72

Data source: Cboe Global Markets.

The win percentage for this very basic approach to selling VIX futures appears to be attractive, with just over 80% of short trades resulting in a profit. Also, the average drawdown is reasonable, at an average move lower of −1.72 VIX points. However, the worst drawdown of −17.60 points should definitely be taken into consideration. In fact, there are four instances where the unrealized loss for shorting VIX futures in this manner tops a 10-point loss. Although these large drawdowns are rare, they are still something that needs to be taken into consideration. Some sort of risk-defined strategy makes a bit more sense when putting on a short trade in response to a spike in VIX.

FUTURES CALENDAR SPREADS

A first alternative to shorting futures would be a calendar spread where the near-dated contract is sold short and the following month contract purchased. This sort of trade reduces the potential profit, but also guards against substantial losses if VIX and the futures contracts continue to rally to higher levels. This approach makes the most sense when the nearer dated month future price moves to a premium relative to the longer dated contract.

Figure 8.2 highlights data from May 29, 2018 and May 30, 2018. The instruments shown in the chart are VIX, the June VIX future, and the July VIX future. On May 29, spot VIX rose by 28.7% to close at 17.02. The June VIX future was up that day as well, rising 12.7% to settle at 15.925. One day later, VIX retraced more than half the rally on May 29 to close at 15.175. If a trader shorted the front month future in reaction to the May 29 price action, they would have made a profit of 0.75.

Figure 8.2: VIX, Jun VIX, and Jul VIX daily prices (May 29–May 30, 2018)

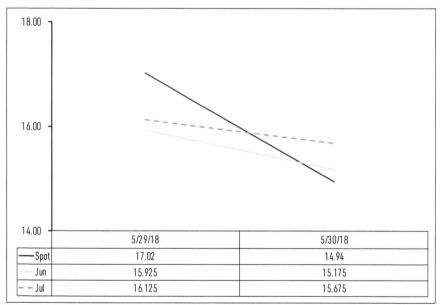

	5/29/18	5/30/18
—— Spot	17.02	14.94
---- Jun	15.925	15.175
– – Jul	16.125	15.675

Data source: Cboe Global Markets.

However, the trader may have chosen to put on a calendar spread where they short the June contract and purchase a July future. They may have chosen this route due to some uncertainty as to whether VIX will remain elevated or possibly rally to higher levels. The calendar spread would combine long the Jun VIX at 15.925 and short the Jul VIX at 16.125. This trade would result in a smaller profit, but one that is somewhat hedged against a big move to the upside. The long leg of the spread would profit 0.75, but the short leg would have given up 0.45 for a net profit of 0.30.

Figure 8.3 shows daily pricing for spot VIX, along with the April and May VIX futures contracts from March 22, 2018 to March 29, 2018. On March 22, VIX was up just over 30% closing at 23.34. The April VIX future was the front month contract at the time and it settled at 19.375, which was a gain of only 11.8%. Note in Figure 8.2 that the April contract is at a pretty significant discount to spot VIX.

Figure 8.3: VIX, Apr VIX, and May VIX daily prices (March 22–March 29, 2018)

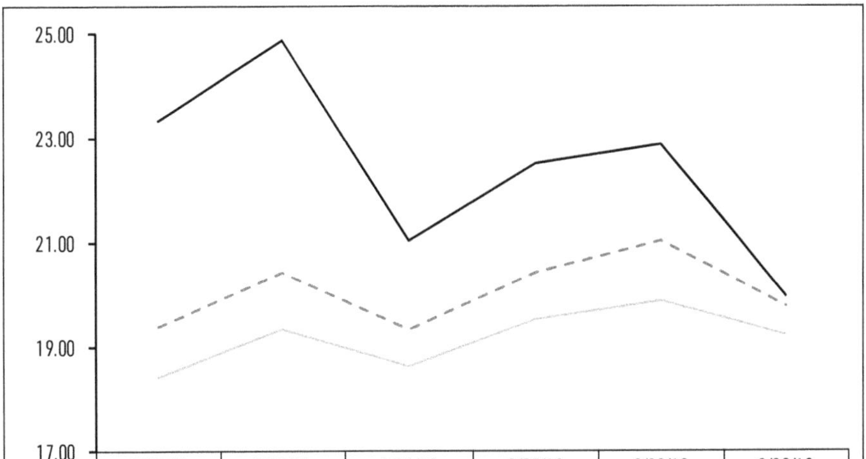

	3/22/18	3/23/18	3/26/18	3/27/18	3/28/18	3/29/18
Spot	23.34	24.87	21.03	22.50	22.87	19.97
Apr	19.375	20.425	19.325	20.425	21.025	19.775
May	18.425	19.325	18.625	19.525	19.875	19.225

Data source: Cboe Global Markets.

In this case it took five trading days for spot VIX to retrace half of the one-day upside move. If a trader had shorted the April contract and held it through this five-day period, they actually would have experienced a loss as the April contract was 0.40 higher five days later. However, note the price action for the May contract over the same time period. It actually rises by 0.80 as the gap between the futures and spot index narrows. In this case, a calendar spread selling April and buying May would have resulted in a small gain. This trade would be a strong consideration due to the wide spread between the futures and spot VIX on the close the day that spot VIX spiked higher.

LONG PUT

Another alternative to shorting futures is purchasing an in-the-money put option with a low amount of time value. There are some distinct advantages to this approach, the major one being that there is a limit to how much a trader can lose when purchasing an option. Buying an option contract and losing the whole premium is never a good outcome, but at least in this case the worst outcome is known. Theoretically, a short VIX futures trade has unlimited losses, which is much more difficult to stomach when the trade is going against you.

To demonstrate the long put in lieu of shorting a future, the VIX spike from May 29, 2018 will be used again. Table 8.4 shows the closing market prices for a variety of June 2018 VIX Put options on that date.

Table 8.4: June 2018 VIX put closing markets on May 29, 2018

Strike	Bid	Ask	Ask time value	Strike	Bid	Ask	Ask time value
19	4.00	4.10	1.025	25	9.40	9.60	0.525
20	4.80	5.00	0.925	26	10.40	10.60	0.525
21	5.70	5.90	0.825	27	11.30	11.50	0.425
22	6.60	6.80	0.725	28	12.30	12.50	0.425
23	7.60	7.70	0.625	29	13.30	13.50	0.425
24	8.50	8.70	0.625	30	14.30	14.40	0.325

Data source: Bloomberg.

Table 8.4 shows the bid and ask prices for several in-the-money VIX put options that expire the same day as the front month futures contract. An extra column is added that shows the time value of each option based on the ask price. This shows the extra premium that would be paid to own a put instead of shorting the VIX future at the settlement price. Note that the deeper in the money the option contract, the lower the time value or extra cost associated with the option. Choosing the correct option is a balance between how much time value there is in the price of the option and the cost of the option, with the cost of the option also being thought of as the risk behind the trade.

This is an example where VIX retraced the one-day move on the following day. Table 8.5 shows the profit based on paying the ask price for each of the put options on May 29 and then selling at the closing bid price on May 30.

Table 8.5: June 2018 VIX put closing ask on May 29 and closing bid on May 30

Strike	5/29 Ask	5/30 Bid	P/L	Strike	5/29 Ask	5/30 Bid	P/L
19	4.10	4.40	0.30	25	9.40	10.00	0.60
20	5.00	5.30	0.30	26	10.40	11.00	0.60
21	5.90	6.20	0.30	27	11.30	12.00	0.70
22	6.80	7.20	0.40	28	12.30	12.90	0.60
23	7.70	8.10	0.40	29	13.30	13.90	0.60
24	8.70	9.10	0.40	30	14.30	14.90	0.60

Data source: Bloomberg.

On May 30, the Jun VIX future dropped by 0.75 to settle at 15.175. The profit, if the various put options were purchased, ranges from 0.30 to 0.70. The deeper in-the-money puts offered a better one-day return, but recall there was a higher price and a follow-through to the upside for these options would have resulted in a potentially larger loss.

VXX BEAR CALL SPREAD

The VXX ETN, discussed more in Chapter 3, usually comes under pressure due to what is referred to as a negative roll yield. The long-term performance for VXX involves a long grind lower with a few upside moves. Those upside moves can be dramatic, but eventually VXX resumes the long-term downtrend that many traders associate with VXX. Because of this, VXX is considered a favorite short candidate, especially when the market is rattled by a volatility spike.

A safe way to play a rally in VXX involves using VXX options for a risk-defined outcome. Specifically, a bear call spread using VXX options is a popular method of getting short volatility without significant exposure if VXX continues to move higher.

VXX was created to match the performance of a strategy index. Specifically, the S&P 500 VIX Short-Term Futures™ Index Total Return. There is data on this index from late 2005. Over this time period, there have been 21 trading days where the index rallied by 15% or more. Typically, the index is lower than this initial move on about 80% of closing observations over four to eight trading days after the initial 15% move. With weekly options available for trading, there is a low risk—but low return—way to take advantage of this. Table 8.6 summarizes the price action for VXX over the following few days.

Table 8.6: VXX closing levels after a 15% one-day price move

Days	Number lower	% lower
4	17	80.95%
5	17	80.95%
6	17	80.95%
7	17	80.95%
9	16	76.19%

Date source: Bloomberg.

Traders who have been involved in the volatility space for some time will not be surprised by these numbers. Typically, VXX loses value and VIX spikes, which results in a quick move up for VXX, which then tends to revert to lower levels over a relatively short period of time. One method of taking advantage of this typical price action for VXX after a 15% spike is by selling a call spread.

Consider "knowing" that there is an 80% chance a security is going to move down over the next few days. In this case, there is an assumption that this historical pattern is going to hold up. Of course, this also means that about one out of five times the trade will not work as planned.

The time periods in Table 8.6 cover five days which all would match up with a VXX expiration date. Table 8.7 highlights which Friday option expiration would be considered for a trade based on which day of the week the 15% spike occurs.

Table 8.7: Appropriate option series based on day of week

Days	Weekday	Option expiration
4	Monday	End of week
5	Friday	End of next week
6	Thursday	End of next week
7	Wednesday	End of next week
9	Tuesday	End of next week

If the upside move occurs on a Monday, then the VXX options that expire at the end of the week would be appropriate for a bear call spread. Any other day of the week and the best series would be the options expiring the following week. The price action for VXX on August 5, 2019 (a Monday) is a good example of how to trade this situation. On this day, VXX closed at 29.30 with the underlying index rising by over 18%. The closing prices for several appropriate call options appear in Table 8.8.

Table 8.8: VXX Aug 9 call option prices on August 5, 2019

Strike price	Close
29.50	1.75
30.00	1.60
30.50	1.45
31.00	1.25
31.50	1.10
32.00	0.95

Data source: Bloomberg.

There are numerous alternatives due to a wide number of option strike prices available for trading. In this case, the VXX Aug 9 29.50 call is sold at 1.75 and the VXX Aug 9 30.50 call is purchased for 1.45 and a net credit of 0.30. If VXX closes at or below 29.50, the result is a profit of 0.30 with both options expiring out of the money. The worst-case scenario is for VXX to continue higher closing over 30.50 which would result in a loss of 0.70. Remember this trade is based on there being an 80% probability that VXX will close under 29.30, and even a small move over 29.30 would result in a 0.30 profit. The worst-case outcome occurs if VXX moves up by about 4% or more over the next four days.

Although it is possible for this trade to result in a partial gain or loss, think about it as having a binary outcome. Either a profit of 0.30 or a loss of 0.70. If history holds up, then this trade should make 0.30 four out of five times the opportunity is traded and lose 0.70 if this is one of the 20% of times it results in a loss. Making 0.30 four times results in a 1.20 profit versus the 0.70 loss that occurs one out of five trades. By no means will a trader become rich waiting around for this short signal, but it does provide a small edge that rarely shows up in the option markets.

When VIX moves up quickly, it more often than not will reverse this move. Due to this mean reversion nature of VIX pricing, the futures contracts will anticipate the spot VIX index moving lower by trading at a discount to spot VIX. The result is that a short trade using VIX futures, options, or ETPs can be a loser, even when spot VIX moves lower.

SUMMARY

- Spot VIX often retraces large upside moves in a short period of time.

- Shorting a volatility spike using VIX-related instruments is a risky method to benefit from this typical price action.

- There are some time periods where a VIX move to the upside is followed by more upside price action.

- With the possibility of VIX continuing to move higher, strategies that have a defined risk are recommended.

9

LONG VOLATILITY TRADES

BEING SHORT volatility can either be a consistent trading strategy acting almost as an investment, or it also works well opportunistically. The previous two chapters demonstrated both approaches to volatility as a tradable asset.

Long volatility is more about trading, specifically keeping the cost of the trade as low as possible while patiently waiting for a pay-off based on a quick move up in volatility. Long volatility is also all about taking profits when the opportunity arises.

This chapter will cover some common strategies used by volatility traders to get long exposure to an increase in expected volatility. Note that the final chapter in this book discusses some of the historical volatility events and looks at how the various trading instruments behaved in response to those stock market sell-offs that resulted in a quick move up in VIX.

LONG FUTURES

In Chapter 5 the beta of VIX futures relative to spot VIX price action was demonstrated based on the number of days remaining until expiration. The closer to expiration, the more closely the VIX future tracks spot VIX. Therefore, if there is the expectation for a very short-term move to the upside in spot VIX, taking a long position in the nearest dated future should be explored. Of course, the number of days remaining may result in the near dated standard future expiration being weeks away. There are VIX futures that expire each week, but as noted earlier, the liquidity may not be quite sufficient.

LONG UNLEVERAGED ETN

There are two general choices with respect to getting exposure to volatility with unleveraged ETPs, either those that focus on the shorter end of the VIX curve or those that focus on the longer end of the curve. These are detailed in Chapter 3, but the short-dated unleveraged long ETPs include VXX or VIXY, while the longer dated ETPs are VXZ and VIXM. Both have performance issues that have been discussed earlier in this book.

Although unleveraged long ETPs have been around since VXX and VXZ were launched in early 2009, there is index data going back to 2005 that shows the performance of these types of ETPs. Based on data integrity, the starting date used for any historical studies related to trading instruments is the beginning of 2007. Using this data, the relationship between the short-dated and long-dated unleveraged ETPs was analyzed to determine what sort of performance can be expected from a long position in either type of ETP. For simplicity's sake, VXX is used to describe the performance of short dated ETPs and VXZ will be used to show the historical performance of the longer dated ETPs.

VXX offers exposure to the front two monthly VIX futures contracts focusing on a 30-calendar-days time frame. In Chapter 4, the beta of VIX futures based on time remaining to expiration was displayed. The beta for a VIX future that has 21 trading days, which often matches up with 30 calendar days, is just under 0.50. It turns out the daily performance of VXX versus VIX results in a beta that is in line with this figure, at 0.49.

VIX OPTION TERM STRUCTURE

VIX options have very high implied volatility when compared to the implied volatility of other markets. As noted earlier, there is a VIX of VIX (VVIX) which oscillates between 80 and 120, with some extremes occurring in both directions. However, VVIX (and VIX for that matter) is a weighted average that does not indicate much about the term structure of options on VIX.

The farther out of the money on the upside, the higher the implied volatility is for VIX options. This means the higher the call strike, the greater the implied volatility as indicated by the price of the option. Figure 9.1 shows a typical term structure for VIX options using pricing of standard December VIX options from November 19, 2018.

Figure 9.1: December 2018 VIX option term structure (November 19, 2018)

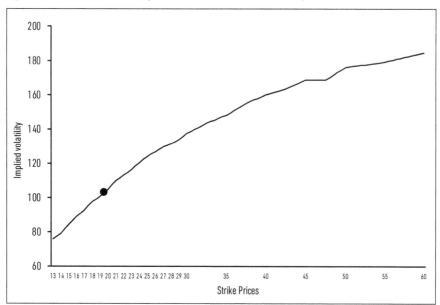

Data source: Bloomberg.

The pricing in Figure 9.1 showing various implied volatility levels uses VIX options that have 30 calendar days remaining to expiration. Spot VIX is at 20.10 and the December VIX Future is priced at 19.375. The 13 puts are the lowest strike used—even though strikes were listed down to 10, the 13 puts were the lowest put strike with both a bid and ask price. Put options pricing up to the 19 strike options is used and then the pricing changes to the call options.

On the upside, all call options up to the 60 strike were used to construct this term structure chart. The 65 and 70 strike options were listed but did not have a bid price so they were excluded from this depiction of the wide range of implied volatility across VIX options sharing an expiration. Usually, a term structure chart is referred to as a "curve," but in this case the shape is more like a line with an upward slope. VVIX closed around 107 that day, near the higher end of its historical range. However, note that the range for the implied volatility of VIX options on this day stretches from just below 80 to almost 200.

The term structure of VIX options means buying out-of-the-money call options results in purchasing an option that has a very high implied volatility. This high implied volatility is justified since VIX and the corresponding futures contracts can move very quickly to the upside. However, this elevated implied volatility also means there is a lot of time value in these options and if an upside move in VIX does not occur, the value of these options could suffer losses in a short period of time. Due to these factors, VIX option traders usually initiate spreads, which allows them to offset some of the time decay and often results in selling options with higher implied volatility than the options that are purchased.

BULL CALL SPREAD

One of the common uses of VIX options to benefit from an upside move is the bull call spread. A bull call spread involves buying a lower strike VIX call and selling a higher strike VIX call with both options sharing an expiration date. When traded in order to benefit from a spike in VIX, both option strike prices are out of the money.

An example of a bull call spread using the December options from the term structure example earlier in this chapter would consist of buying the VIX Dec 23 Call for 1.40 and selling the VIX Dec 28 Call at 0.70 for a net cost of 0.70. At this time, the December future was trading at 19.40 and spot VIX was at 20.10. Also, the December future and options had 30 days remaining to expiration. Figure 9.2 shows the pay-off for this bull call spread if held through December settlement.

Figure 9.2: VIX Dec 23/28 bull call spread pay-off at December settlement

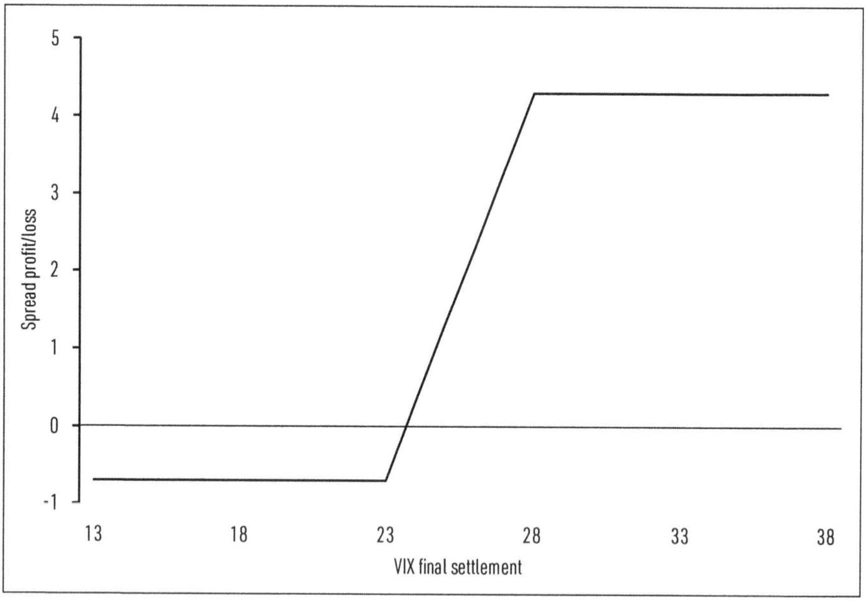

Data source: Bloomberg.

Most option traders will recognize this payout diagram representing a bullish vertical spread. The best-case scenario for a vertical spread is to hold the trade through expiration to get the maximum value out of the spread, especially if the underlying market appears to be on track to close above the higher strike. In this case, the spread cost 0.70 and at expiration if December VIX settlement is above 28.00 the trade will result in a profit of 4.30. At any settlement price at or above 28.00 the 23 strike call will be worth 5.00 more than the 28 strike call. Subtracting the cost of the spread (0.70) from the value of the spread results in a profit of 4.30.

The issue with this is that VIX tends to spike to higher levels, holding those levels for a short period of time, before then reverting to a lower price. To benefit from a long volatility trade, profits will almost always need to be realized when a market event pushes VIX quickly to higher levels. There were 30 calendar days remaining until December settlement when the spread was priced at 0.70. Figure 9.3 shows the profit and loss at settlement, but adds an estimate of where the VIX Dec 23/28 bull call spread would be valued at various underlying prices with 15 days remaining to VIX settlement.

Figure 9.3: VIX Dec 23/28 bull call spread pay-off 15 days before and at December settlement

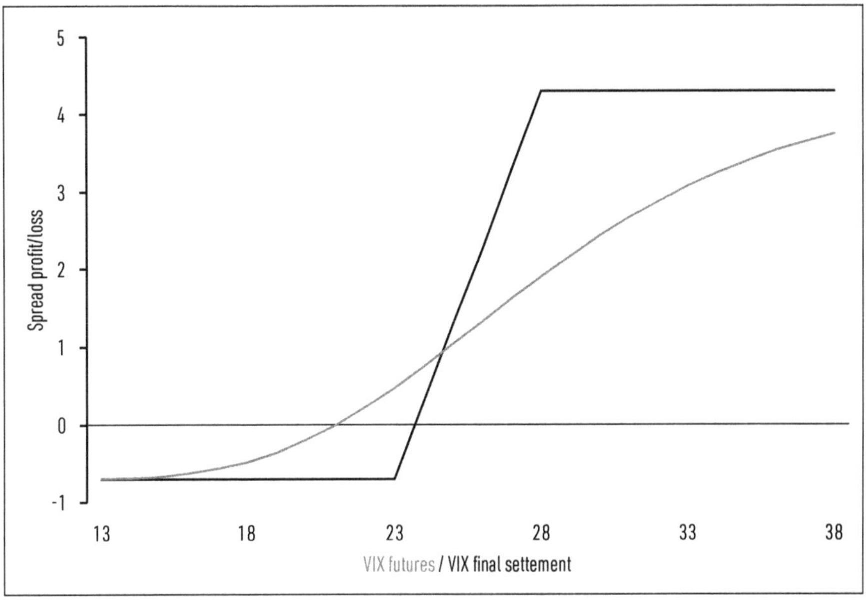

Data source: Bloomberg.

The lighter colored, curved line estimates the profit and loss for the bull call spread at various December VIX futures prices with 15 days remaining until expiration. Recall VIX options are best priced off the VIX future that shares an expiration date. Also, when the options were priced to create the spread, the 28 call prices indicated an implied volatility around 135% and the 23 call priced in 115% implied volatility. This 20-point spread between the two is assumed to determine the pay-off at 15 days.

There are a few things to note about the 15 days to expiration pay-off. First, the trade is actually in profit with the December VIX future trading below the lower strike option. Also, the maximum 0.70 loss is not reached unless the December VIX future is around 15.00. The biggest difference between the payout at expiration and 15 days until expiration pay-off is apparent on the upside. For instance, if the December VIX future is at 28.00 the spread profit is estimated to be 1.90, much lower than the 4.30 potential profit that could happen at expiration. Table 9.1 covers some key levels for this bull call spread based on various five-day increments until December settlement.

Table 9.1: Profit/loss and break-even levels for VIX Dec 23/28 bull call spread

Days to expiration	P/L at 19.40	P/L at 23.00	P/L at 28.00	Break-even
0	−0.70	−0.70	4.30	23.70
5	−0.57	0.33	2.64	22.05
10	−0.40	0.46	2.19	21.40
15	−0.30	0.48	1.90	21.00
20	−0.24	0.47	1.71	20.80
25	−0.20	0.45	1.55	20.70

Data source: Bloomberg.

Remember the December VIX future was trading at 19.40 when this spread was priced. Therefore, this price level is included to show the time decay of this spread. With the December future price at 23.00, this spread would show a profit, even with just five days remaining until expiration. Also, the closer to December expiration, the greater the profit if there is a December VIX future price spike to 28.00. Finally, the break-even levels for this spread show that a move higher, but not quite to the lower strike price of 23, could result in a small profit for this trade.

BULL CALL SPREAD PLUS SHORT PUT

VIX traders are an innovative bunch and the bull call spread is popular, but these traders have expanded on ways to lower the cost of long volatility exposure. One method is to sell an out-of-the-money put to lower the cost of the overall spread.

Two examples of how the bull call spread from the previous section can be supplemented with a short put will be demonstrated, with one being a bit more aggressive than the other. First, a less aggressive example would involve buying the VIX Dec 23 Call for 1.40, selling the VIX Dec 28 Call for 0.70, and then finally selling a VIX Dec 15 Call for 0.30. This lowers the cost of the trade from 0.70 to 0.40 and also changes the pay-off structure as well. Figure 9.4 shows the pay-off at December expiration for this short put plus bull call spread.

Figure 9.4: Short VIX Dec 15 put + VIX Dec 23/28 bull call spread pay-off at settlement

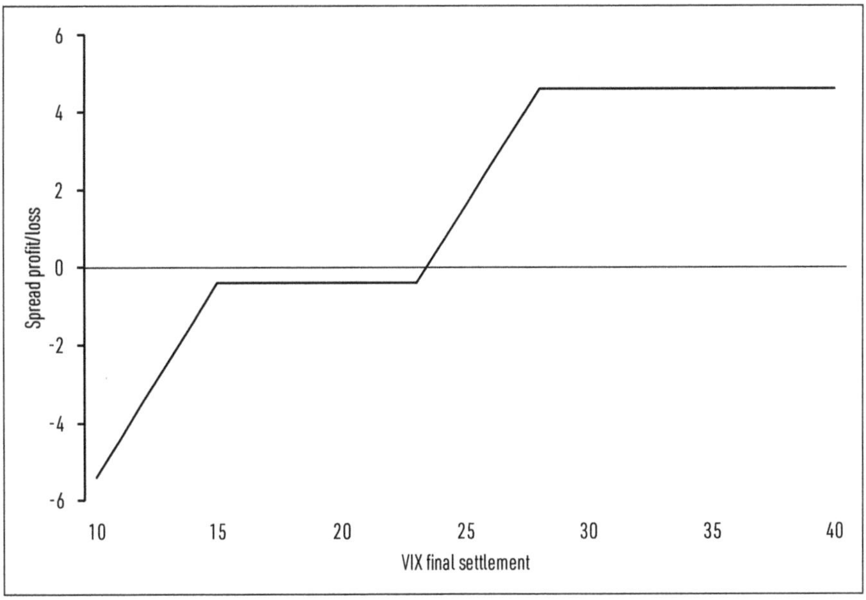

Data source: Bloomberg.

There are extra moving parts to this trade, which changes the potential pay-off based on different times until expiration. Figure 9.5 adds a component showing the potential pay-off based on various levels for the Dec VIX future at different levels. The pay-off is somewhat linear between 20.00 and 35.00. Below 20, losses begin to accelerate and above 35 the pay-off starts to flatten out.

Figure 9.5: Short VIX Dec 15 Put + VIX Dec 23/28 bull call spread pay-off 15 days before and at December settlement

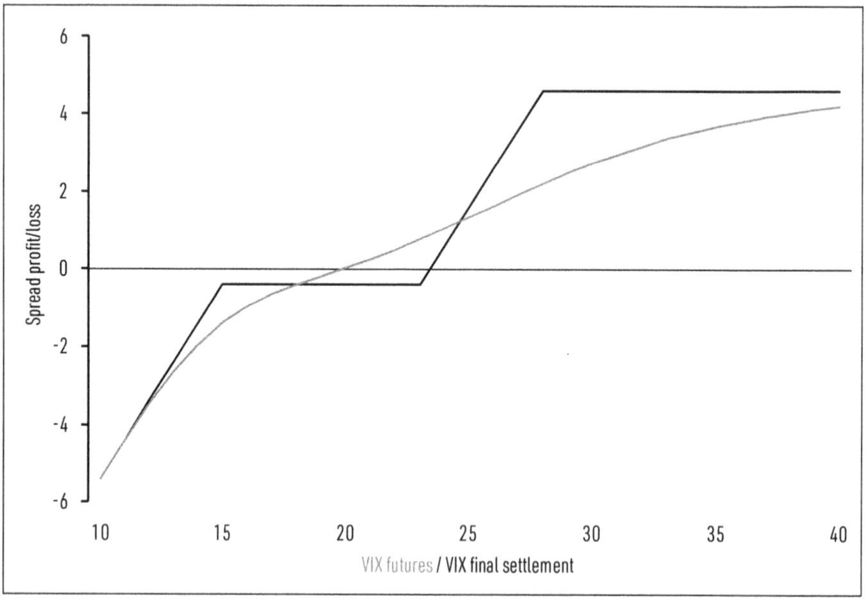

Data source: Bloomberg.

This type of spread will hold a good portion of value if the futures contract remains around 19.40. At 10 days to expiration, if the future is at 19.40 the trade should show about a 0.13 unrealized loss. At 15 days and longer the trade shows an unrealized loss of less than 0.10.

Table 9.2 covers several time frames and several price levels over the life of the trade. In addition to the trade holding value over a good portion of the time to expiration, it also maintains a break-even price level of around 20.00 until about 10 days to expiration. Finally, a quick move to 23.00 results in a profit of around 0.75 in the period between 10 and 20 days to expiration.

Table 9.2: Profit/loss and break-even levels for short VIX Dec 15 Put + VIX Dec 23/28 bull call spread

Days to expiration	P/L at 10.00	P/L at 15.00	P/L at 19.40	P/L at 23.00	P/L at 28.00	Break-even
0	−5.40	−0.40	−0.40	−0.40	4.60	23.40
5	−5.40	−0.99	−0.28	0.63	2.95	21.05
10	−5.40	−1.22	−0.13	0.76	2.49	20.10
15	−5.40	−1.39	−0.08	0.78	2.21	19.75
20	−5.40	−1.52	−0.09	0.75	2.00	19.75
25	−5.40	−1.63	−0.13	0.70	1.85	19.95

Data source: Bloomberg.

A more aggressive version of this trade would sell a higher strike put option, specifically a higher strike put option that would result in the trade taking in a credit when the spread is implemented. In this case, the VIX Dec 17 Put could be sold for 0.90, which combined with the 0.70 cost of the Dec 23/28 bull call spread results in a credit of 0.20.

Figure 9.6: Short VIX Dec 17 Put + VIX Dec 23/28 bull call spread pay-off at settlement

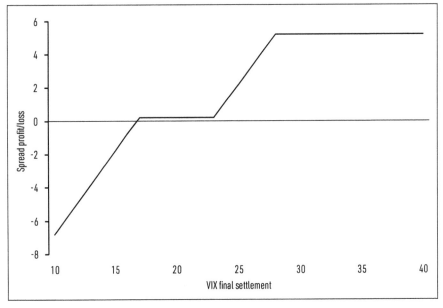

Data source: Bloomberg.

This more aggressive version of shorting a put and buying a call spread is attractive to traders because it results in a profit at expiration if VIX remains unchanged or even loses a small amount of value. It also holds value relative to the passage of time. This shows up in Figure 9.7, which adds the estimated profit or loss of this trade with 15 days remaining to expiration.

Figure 9.7: Short VIX Dec 17 put + VIX Dec 23/28 bull call spread pay-off 15 days before and at December settlement

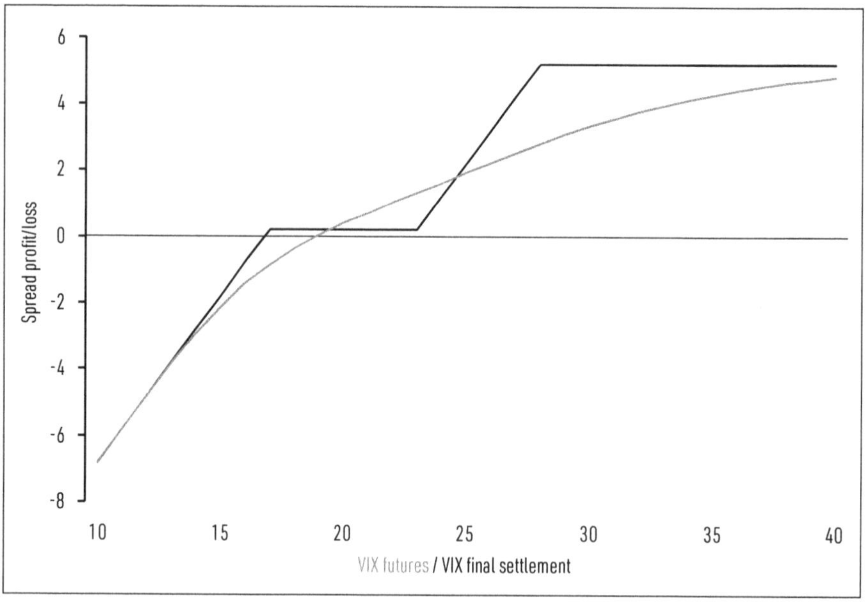

Data source: Bloomberg.

Recall the VIX future was trading just over 19.00 when this trade would be implemented. Fifteen days later, if the underlying market has not changed in price, this trade will actually be in a small profit. A spread like this works well when targeting a specific event.

For instance, for a few years there was a version of this trade that was executed the day before the monthly employment report and taken off regardless of the reaction in the market the following day. The trade would be exited for a small loss if the employment number did not have a negative impact on the stock market, or a profit would be realized if VIX moved higher based on a weak stock market reaction to the number.

The trade is more aggressive than the version that shorts the 15 put, but over the life of the trade it would show a small profit if the futures price remained where it was when the trade was implemented. Note the P/L is always positive if the futures price maintains the 19.40 level.

Table 9.3: Profit/loss and break-even levels for short VIX Dec 15 put + VIX Dec 23/28 bull call spread

Days to expiration	P/L at 10.00	P/L at 17.00	P/L at 19.40	P/L at 23.00	P/L at 28.00	Break-even
0	−6.80	0.20	0.20	0.20	5.20	16.80
5	−6.80	−0.46	0.25	1.23	3.55	18.25
10	−6.80	−0.68	0.27	1.34	3.09	18.60
15	−6.80	−0.83	0.21	1.33	2.81	18.85
20	−6.80	−0.96	0.12	1.26	2.60	19.10
25	−6.80	−1.08	0.02	1.17	2.43	19.35

Data source: Bloomberg.

One of the beneficial things about this final spread that takes in a credit is that it holds value if VIX does not change much in value. This results in a spread that offers a hedge against a stock market drop, but does not result in a drag on performance. Also, this type of position is often rolled close to expiration, allowing a firm to have some tail risk protection at little cost or even a small profit.

Long volatility exposure is usually a costly prospect. This shows up in the consistent underperformance of long VIX-related ETPs. In most market environments, VIX futures contracts also come under price pressure unless there is some sort of quick move up in spot VIX and even then, the futures move will lag that of the spot index. Option spreads are useful ways to benefit from a VIX spike, but at the same time they do not give up too much performance if the spike does not materialize.

SUMMARY

- Long volatility trading with VIX instruments often appears to be an expensive trade.

- VIX futures are usually at a premium to spot VIX and a spike may result in VIX rising to a larger extent than the future.

- This aspect of the futures pricing impacts VIX options price activity as well.

- Also, VIX call option implied volatility usually increases as the strike prices move higher.

- Long VIX-related ETPs are another alternative to being long volatility, but they suffer from negative roll yield which makes them most appropriate for short term trades.

10
SPREAD TRADING WITH VOLATILITY FUTURES

CALENDAR SPREADS are very popular in the commodity futures space where traders take advantage of various seasonal trends. For example, taking a long position in May Corn and a short position in September Corn if there is a belief that the spread between the two contract prices will widen, with May rising relative to the September contract price.

There are also commodity-related futures trades that pair two similar markets together, such as WTI and Brent Oil contracts. The common practice in this case would be to trade contracts that share an expiration month based on their expected relative performance.

The price behavior of VIX futures contracts lends itself to trading different expirations against each other. Specifically, shorting a near dated contract while buying a longer dated contract when a normal contango-like shape is priced in by VIX futures. This sort of trade would be similar to the short-term trades highlighted in Chapter 7, but the expectation would be that the nearer dated future would lose more value than a longer dated contract, as opposed to just having a short position in the shorter dated contract.

The VSTOXX futures that trade in Europe offer a comparable contract that may be traded against VIX futures in a similar manner to two similar contracts that offer exposure to slightly different oil prices. Sometimes the expectations for volatility in Europe may be elevated versus similar expectations in the US. The result is opportunities to take a long position in one market and a short position in the other with the expectation that this relationship will shift over time.

CALENDAR SPREADS

A couple of examples of VIX futures calendar spreads were discussed in Chapter 7 as a response to quick moves to the upside in VIX. In those examples, the front month was sold short and the second month purchased. The goal was for the front month future to lose more value than the long second month position when spot VIX moved to lower levels.

The exercise that dominated Chapter 7 on consistently shorting volatility is repeated in this chapter to highlight how a consistent strategy selling a front month future and buying the second month would work as expiration for the front month future approaches. Every standard expiration from January 2007 to 2019 was used for this set of tests. Only the standard futures contracts were used for this set of tests and an extra screening technique was introduced.

Table 10.1 shows the results from a strategy that sells the front month future and buys the second month future based on a certain number of days to expiration. The trade would be exited the night before the front month future expires.

Table 10.1: Selling month 1/buying month 2 future and exiting day before expiration

Days to expiration	Total points	Observations	Spread profitable	% Spread profitable	Maximum profit	Maximum loss	Average profit
9	32.27	156	94	60.26%	5.62	−5.55	0.21
8	35.97	156	92	58.97%	9.40	−5.41	0.23
7	36.37	156	87	55.77%	5.57	−5.91	0.23
6	28.35	156	92	58.97%	3.35	−5.00	0.18
5	41.90	156	99	63.46%	6.48	−5.23	0.27
4	30.32	156	100	64.10%	12.10	−5.17	0.19
3	20.95	156	88	56.41%	7.21	−4.40	0.13
2	7.27	156	87	55.77%	2.28	−2.70	0.05

Data source: Bloomberg.

This method of systematically selling the front month and buying the second month future works fairly well given that there is no consideration regarding the volatility environment or relative pricing. A key figure to focus on is the biggest loss, which never tops 6 points. When testing for just selling the front month individually many of the losses came in at over 20 points for a single trade.

The next test screens out situations where the front month is trading at a discount to spot VIX. This is the same screen that was utilized as a filter in the tests run in Chapter 7. Table 10.2 shows these results.

Table 10.2: Selling month 1/buying month 2 future when month 1 is higher than spot VIX

Days to expiration	Total points	Observations	Spread profitable	% Spread profitable	Maximum profit	Maximum loss	Average profit
9	27.82	118	72	61.02%	2.15	−4.50	0.24
8	14.35	128	72	56.25%	3.45	−5.41	0.11
7	11.99	120	64	53.33%	2.45	−4.45	0.10
6	20.41	118	68	57.63%	2.15	−2.94	0.17
5	23.86	113	69	61.06%	1.90	−3.38	0.21
4	22.47	120	80	66.67%	2.30	−2.20	0.19
3	10.14	126	71	56.35%	2.21	−3.00	0.08
2	2.43	100	55	55.00%	1.00	−2.70	0.02

Data source: Bloomberg.

Filtering out observations where the front month is lower than spot VIX has mixed results. The maximum loss taken over the 13-year period is reduced, but so is the maximum profit. The average profit ranges from 0.02 to 0.24, but there is no real pattern present with respect to how many days are remaining to expiration.

A new filter implemented in this situation looked at the front month versus the second month future. It may be counterintuitive, but the trade would only be implemented when the front month is lower than the second month. This is more in line with a normal VIX term structure. These results are shown in Table 10.3.

Table 10.3: Selling month 1/buying month 2 future when month 1 is lower than month 2

Days to expiration	Total points	Observations	Spread profitable	% Spread profitable	Maximum profit	Maximum loss	Average profit
9	12.43	122	71	58.20%	2.85	−5.55	0.10
8	16.15	126	73	57.94%	2.20	−5.41	0.13
7	14.91	124	67	54.03%	2.45	−5.91	0.12
6	18.29	121	73	60.33%	1.75	−5.00	0.15
5	18.12	126	79	62.70%	2.55	−5.23	0.14
4	10.94	125	80	64.00%	2.05	−5.17	0.09
3	12.16	122	71	58.20%	1.85	−2.00	0.10
2	8.67	121	67	55.37%	1.15	−1.75	0.07

Data source: Bloomberg.

Screening with just the relative VIX futures prices did not result in much improvement. In fact, it appears that this approach would be a bit worse than blindly putting on a calendar spread as expiration approaches.

A final test was run where the trade would only be done if spot VIX is lower than the front month future and the front month future is lower than the second month future. Again, this may be a bit counterintuitive as this involves selling a lower price future and buying a higher price one, but the goal is to benefit from this spread widening, which would be expected as expiration approaches. The results of this approach appear in Table 10.4.

Table 10.4: Selling month 1/buying month 2 future when VIX is lower than month 1 and month 1 is lower than month 2

Days to expiration	Total points	Observations	Spread profitable	% Spread profitable	Maximum profit	Maximum loss	Average profit
9	41.74	104	69	66.35%	2.15	−2.05	0.40
8	38.73	107	68	63.55%	2.20	−2.10	0.36
7	29.11	104	60	57.69%	2.45	−2.10	0.28
6	32.29	103	65	63.11%	1.75	−1.85	0.31
5	28.97	101	65	64.36%	1.90	−1.70	0.29
4	32.83	105	76	72.38%	2.30	−1.55	0.31
3	19.88	109	67	61.47%	1.85	−2.00	0.18
2	8.19	87	48	55.17%	1.00	−1.10	0.09

Data source: Bloomberg.

The final approach appears to be the best of the four tests. The average profit is fairly consistent from four days and longer to expiration, and the maximum losses at worst are slightly over 2.00. The win percentage improves over all time periods, especially with four days remaining to expiration.

These systematic approaches can be expanded on through further filters or more dynamic stop loss levels. However, the results here are a good first step toward a systematic approach to trading VIX calendar spreads.

Both long and short volatility trades may benefit by combining VIX futures expirations. The most basic of long volatility trades would involve buying a front month future. However, the downside to this sort of trade is that, when the future is at a premium to the index, which is the majority of trading days, the spread between the spot index and the future will narrow. This may be thought of in the same way that time decay takes value out of an option contract.

When traders are concerned about option time decay they will look for an option to sell to offset some of that time decay. This is the same idea behind using a calendar spread for long VIX exposure. If VIX does not rally, the front month future may lose value over time. If a trader buys the front month future and shorts the second month contract, they will have a position that will offset some of the price decline in the front month future.

Often when there is a volatility spike the front month future will move up more than the second month future. The second month future will move up as well, but usually not at the same rate as the front month future. In order for the VIX term structure to move from contango to backwardation, the front month future will need to move up more than the second month contract. When this occurs, the long front month, short second month calendar spread will still make a profit. Of course, the profit will not be as great as what would be realized by just owning the front month contract, but the risk of loss would be reduced.

On September 4, 2019 VIX closed at 17.33, the Sep VIX (M01) future settled at 18.075, and the Oct (M02) contract settlement price was 18.675. VIX had been approaching higher levels and then backing off. Based on the price action, a trader decides they want long exposure to VIX through the middle of September, conveniently coinciding with September 17, which is the day before September VIX settlement. They decide to narrow their trade down to two choices. Either buy the Sep VIX future or put on a calendar spread buying the September contract and shorting the October contract. Figure 10.1 shows the two choices using the settlement prices for each.

Figure 10.1: Long Sep VIX versus long Sep VIX/short Oct VIX (2019)

Trade 1: Buy Sep VIX future at 18.075

Trade 2: Buy Sep VIX future at 18.075/Sell Oct VIX future at 18.675

Data source: Cboe Global Markets.

This trade is not going to work, but is being used as an example of how some losses may be offset by selling the second month future. Over the nine trading days between September 4 and September 17, VIX and both futures contracts grind lower. By the close on September 17, VIX is down 2.89, the Sep VIX future has lost 3.55, and the Oct VIX future is down 1.60. Figure 10.2 shows the running day-to-day losses for Trade 1 (long future) and Trade 2 (calendar spread).

Figure 10.2: Daily P/L for long Sep VIX and long Sep/short Oct VIX trades (2019)

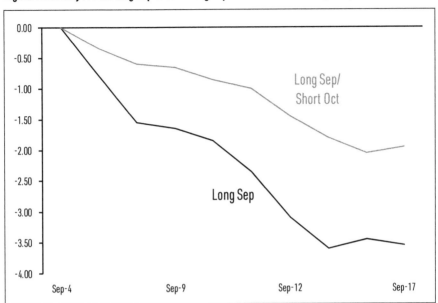

Data source: Cboe Global Markets.

Again, over this time period spot VIX was down 2.89. The September future lost more than 2.89 as the premium between the future and index narrowed as expiration approached. The calendar spread position was not a winner, but the losses were much less than for a pure long position.

A second example combines a long position in the near month and short position in the second month in anticipation of a spike in volatility. On August 1, 2019 VIX closed at 17.87, up 1.75 from the previous day. The front month August contract settled at 17.475 and the September future settlement price was 17.775. A trader who believes this move may continue might consider buying the August contract and selling the September future. Table 10.5 shows the performance of this spread trade over the next seven trading days.

Table 10.5: Daily P/L for long Aug VIX/short Sep VIX trade

Day	VIX	Aug	Sep	Spread P/L
0	17.87	17.475	17.775	N/A
1	17.61	17.475	17.675	0.10
2	24.59	21.625	20.225	1.70
3	20.17	19.675	19.425	0.55
4	19.49	19.375	19.125	0.55
5	16.91	17.725	18.075	−0.05
6	17.97	18.475	18.575	0.20
7	21.09	20.775	19.975	1.10

Data source: Cboe Global Markets.

This period of time included a few days where the August contract closed at a premium to the September contract as VIX moved up and pushed the short end of the curve into backwardation. This calendar spread did well over a few days, but fell back into unprofitable levels very quickly as VIX displayed the normal reversion to a mean price behavior that is common after a quick move higher.

VSTOXX VERSUS VIX

Another form of futures spread trading may combine VSTOXX futures with VIX futures contracts. There are times when volatility expectations are elevated in one market versus another. One example shows up in Chapter 11, where the Brexit referendum pushed the VSTOXX index to elevated levels versus VIX as the date of the vote approached.

VSTOXX is typically at a premium to VIX with the average close for VSTOXX from 2010 to 2019 around 23.72, and the average VIX close at 19.72 over the same period of time. Both do tend to move in the same direction. Figure 10.3 shows the daily closing pricing for both volatility indexes on days that both markets were open in 2019.

Figure 10.3: Daily closing prices for VIX and VSTOXX (2019)

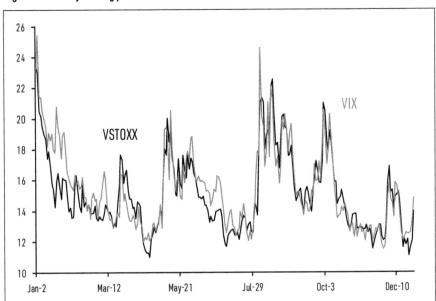

Data source: Bloomberg.

Over the course of the year, VSTOXX and VIX closing prices tend to trend together and the difference periodically widens out and converges. The futures contracts will do the same as well, but often not to the same extent. Figure 10.4 shows the relative price difference between the two indexes and the front month June futures contracts for each over a three-week period in late May to mid-June 2019.

Figure 10.4: Daily closing price difference for VIX and VSTOXX indexes and futures (2019)

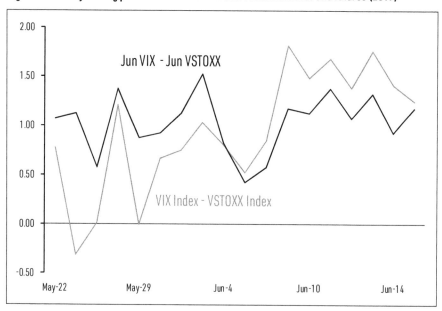

Data source: Bloomberg.

Figure 10.4 shows the level of the difference between spot VIX and VSTOXX indexes as VIX minus VSTOXX. At this time, VIX was at a premium to VSTOXX the majority of trading days. This difference ranged from VIX closing 1.82 higher than VSTOXX, and VIX closing at a 0.31 discount to VSTOXX. The difference between the futures contracts is also displayed by subtracting the June VSTOXX future price from the June VIX future close. The range here is a little narrower with VIX as low as a 0.50 premium to as high as a 1.50 premium.

The closing times for the two indexes and the futures contracts are different, so changes in one market when the other is not open may cause this spread to vary. Also, keep in mind that VSTOXX futures have a multiplier of 100 euros while the VIX futures multiplier is 1,000 USD. An effective spread trade would need to take into account this multiplier difference, as well as the exchange range between the US dollar and euro currency.

SUMMARY

- Calendar spreads using VIX futures contracts are a very popular method of trading the VIX term structure.

- A calendar spread may reduce the risk associated with a volatility spike that would negatively impact a pure short volatility trade.

- VIX and VSTOXX futures share a price relationship that favors spread trades when their spread moves outside of historical norms.

PART III

HISTORIC VOLATILITY EVENTS

11

VOLATILITY EVENTS

NOTHING CATCHES headlines like a sell-off in the stock markets. Historically, these sell-offs have been associated with a quick rise in VIX. In fact, if you are watching your favorite business network, and the S&P 500 (SPX) is off several percentage points, the next thing the commentator will cite is what VIX is up to. A common term for these instances is a "volatility event."

If you are considering trading volatility derivatives, it is valuable to be familiar with how VIX has reacted during these volatility events. VIX can move dramatically in a short period of time and the derivatives associated with VIX can jump in price as well. Being aware of how much VIX may move in a day, how high it can go, and how long it may stay at elevated levels are all pieces of information that help traders navigate these somewhat rare, but significant, market events.

In this chapter, I survey the following major historic volatility events and describe the VIX action: 1987 stock market crash; Asian flu, 1997; Russian financial crisis, 1998; September 11, 2001; Great Financial Crisis; flash crash; European sovereign debt crisis, 2011; Black Monday, 2015; Brexit referendum; election of Donald Trump; inflation in employment number, 2018; and global pandemic, 2020. I begin with the market crash of 1987.

STOCK MARKET CRASH, 1987

The stock market crash of 1987 was a perfect storm of events. It may have been the first time global markets moved in sync, which showed traders just how interconnected the global markets had become. The sell-off in the US occurred on a Monday. However, hours before, stock selling commenced in Asia, then moved to Europe—and then landed in the US.

When the dust settled on October 19, 1987 or "Black Monday," the S&P 500 had lost just over 20%. A bear market is defined by a drop of 20% and this happened on a single trading day. This large price drop came on the heels of a 5% sell-off the previous Friday, which was the first 5% drop for the S&P 500 since May of 1962.

There is no VIX data from before 1990, but there was a predecessor to VIX quoted using the ticker VXO. VXO is still calculated and quoted by Cboe Global Markets. VXO uses a methodology that is similar to how VIX is calculated. It is calculated using pricing from the S&P 100 index (OEX), which was the most active broad-based index option market at the time. The VXO data in this section was not available in real time, but was calculated after the fact. Finally, it is worth noting that the OEX option market was considered a contributor to the extent of the Black Monday sell-off.

LEADING UP TO BLACK MONDAY

The S&P 500 peaked in 1987 on August 25, up 39% for the year. This followed a rise of 14.6% in 1986. Volatility indexes are always relative and the average for VXO from the first day of the year through August 25 was 22.51, while the average VXO close in 1986 was 20.41. Despite the very bullish move for stocks, option volatility was much higher leading up to the highest stock market close for the year. Figure 11.1 shows the relative performance of VXO and the S&P 500 during this tremendous bull run.

Figure 11.1: Daily VXO pricing (January 2–August 25, 1987)

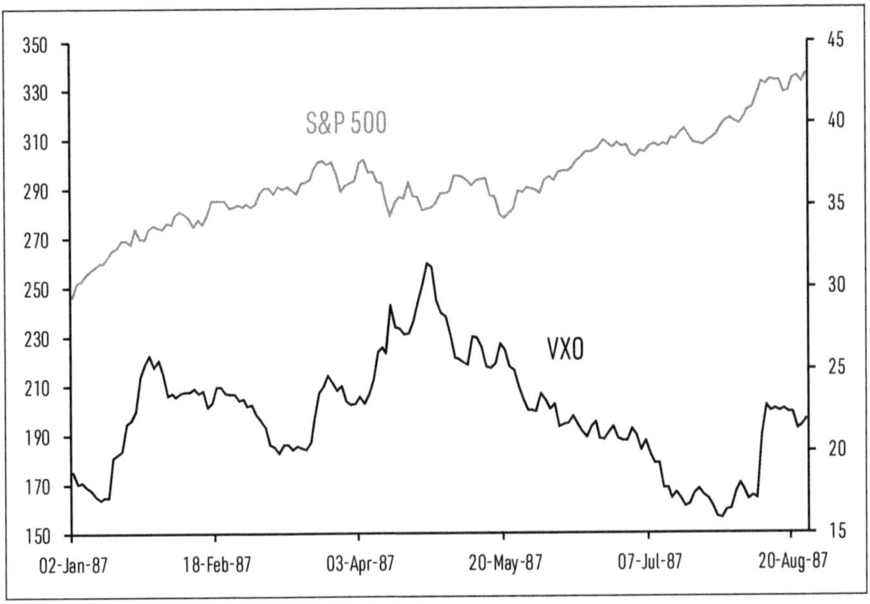

Data sources: Bloomberg and Cboe Global Markets.

About two weeks before the peak of the stock market, VXO jumped tremendously, rising from 17.09 on August 10 to 20.91 on August 11. This was in conjunction with a rise of 1.6% in the S&P 500 over the same one-day period. The news of the day involved the US firing at an Iranian jet, which didn't rattle the stock markets but may have boosted volatility expectations.

Figure 11.2 takes a look at how the S&P 500 and VXO behaved from the peak of the stock market on August 25 through the Friday before Black Monday.

Figure 11.2: Daily VXO pricing (August 25–October 16, 1987)

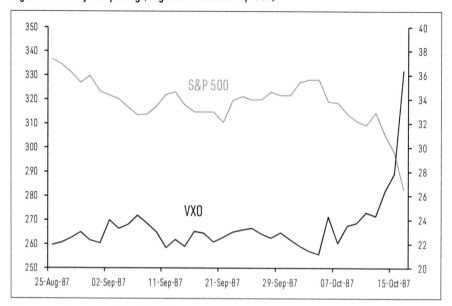

Data sources: Bloomberg and Cboe Global Markets.

With the exception of the days just before the crash, the price action for both the S&P 500 and VXO is relatively unremarkable. VXO bounced between 21 and 24, while the S&P 500 was fairly range bound. A couple of data points do stand out.

On October 12 VXO closed at 24.59. This was a new recent high for the volatility index and this occurred as the S&P 500 closed just under 310. A few days before this, on October 7, VXO closed at 24.28. This was the first breach of the 24 level since early September (September 8) and also was in reaction to a higher S&P 500 close than occurred in September. This slight divergence may have been a precursor to lower stock prices on the horizon.

Figure 11.3 shows the S&P 500 and VXO price action for the last four months of 1987, a period of time that covers just before and after the stock market sell-off on October 19. VXO closed at 150.19 on Black Monday, up from 36.37 on Friday, October 16.

Figure 11.3: Daily VXO pricing (September–December 1987)

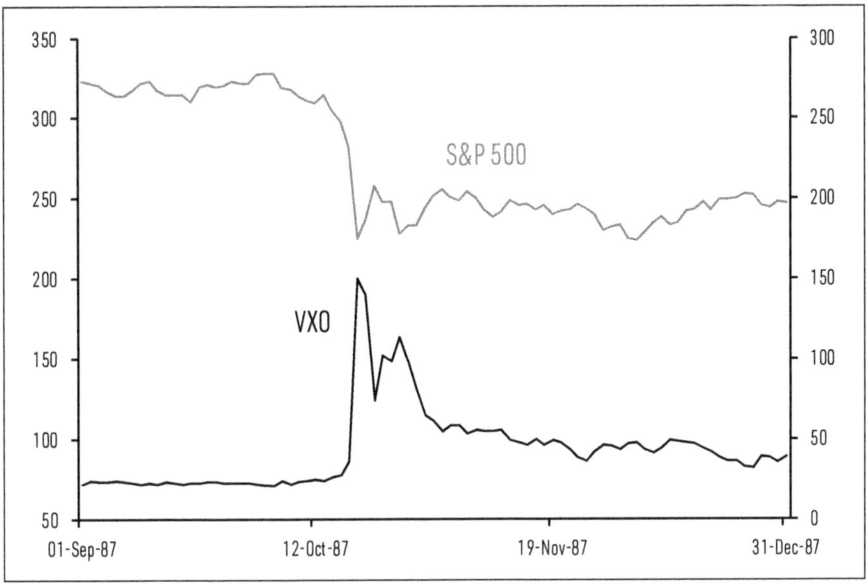

Data sources: Bloomberg and Cboe Global Markets.

The fallout from Black Monday stuck with the option market for a while. The lowest VXO close in 1987 following Black Monday was 31.65, and VXO did not manage to close below 20 until July of the following year. Table 11.1 shows the daily percent change for the S&P 500 and corresponding VXO close each day for the two weeks including and following Black Monday.

Table 11.1: Daily S&P 500 changes and VXO closes (October 16–October 30, 1987)

Date	S&P 500 close	Daily change	VXO close
10/19/1987	224.84	−20.47%	150.19
10/20/1987	236.83	5.33%	140.00
10/21/1987	258.38	9.10%	73.91
10/22/1987	248.25	−3.92%	102.22
10/23/1987	248.22	−0.01%	98.81
10/26/1987	227.67	−8.28%	113.33
10/27/1987	233.19	2.42%	97.51
10/28/1987	233.28	0.04%	81.24
10/29/1987	244.77	4.93%	64.66
10/30/1987	251.79	2.87%	61.41

Data sources: Bloomberg and Cboe Global Markets.

Another longer term adjustment to option prices was the relative pricing of index options. Before Black Monday, a term structure chart showing the various individual options implied would curve upward as strike prices moved both lower and higher than the current market price. After the crash of 1987, the shape of this curve was permanently altered with the implied volatility for strike prices lower than the current market moving up more quickly than the implied volatility for options with strike prices higher than the current market price. Figure 11.4 is a very basic illustration of an option skew chart.

Figure 11.4: SPX volatility term structure, before and after Black Monday

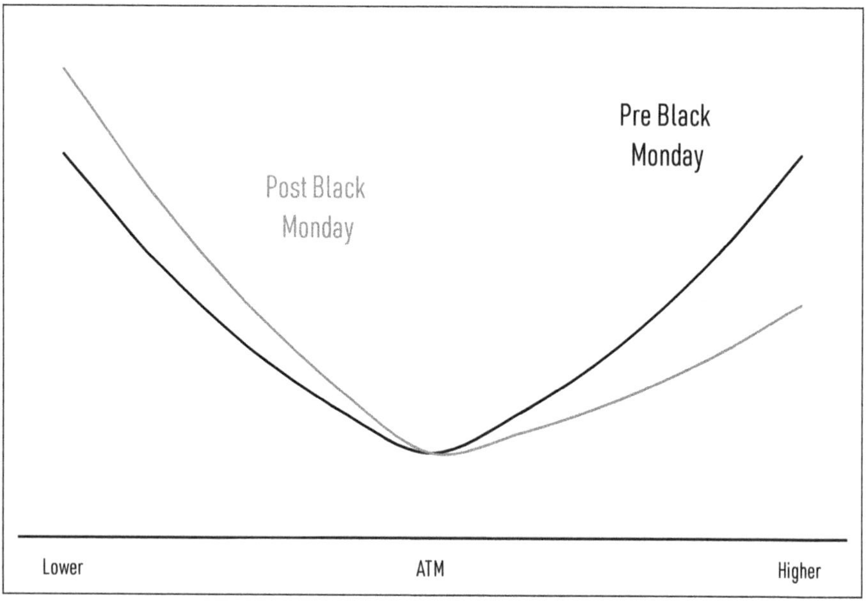

Data sources: Bloomberg and Cboe Global Markets.

The dark line in Figure 11.4 represents the general shape of the volatility skew for index options such as the S&P 100 at that time. The shape usually resembled a "smile," where the implied volatility for out-of-the-money puts and calls rose symmetrically. October 1987 was a reminder that markets go down much quicker than they rise. This reminder resulted in a permanent shift in the shape of this curve. Out-of-the-money put implied volatility remained permanently higher than comparable out-of-the-money call volatility and the result of this adjustment is a permanent shift in the typical curve to something that is skewed to the downside.

OBSERVATIONS

Black Monday was a game changer, a shock to the financial markets. It saw the kind of price action that had not been experienced in decades.

In the midst of the market implosion of 2008, the closing high for VIX was 80.86 (VXO reached 87.24) and the peak for VIX during the coronavirus pandemic in 2020 was 82.69 (VXO topped 90 at 93.85). Anyone that traded through either or both of those periods of time can only fathom what VIX in the 150s would feel like. Many market participants think of the '80s as the ceiling for VIX; however, using a longer look-back period pushes that number well over 100.

ASIAN FLU, OCTOBER 1997

On October 27, 1997 the S&P 500 dropped 6.9%, which was the biggest one-day decline since the period around the crash of 1987. In fact, due to circuit breaker rules that were in place at the time, the NYSE closed 30 minutes before the normal market closing time of 4:00 pm Eastern. Note that this was before the availability of 24-hour derivative instruments, which now allow traders exposure to the US stock market around the clock.

What is interesting about this sudden decline on October 27 is that the Asian flu story had been playing out over the course of weeks, beginning with speculative activity in the currency of Thailand, the baht. On July 2, 1997 the baht was allowed to float versus the US dollar, which eventually resulted in a 50% drop in the value of the currency. This story was playing out over time and didn't hit the US until almost four months later.

There was some interesting VIX versus SPX price action as the crisis was unfolding. VIX typically drops—or at least does not rise—when the S&P 500 is moving higher. However, in the summer of 1997 VIX moved up in sync with the S&P 500. Figure 11.5 shows the daily closing prices for both VIX and SPX from May through September 1997.

Figure 11.5: Daily VIX and SPX pricing (May–September 1997)

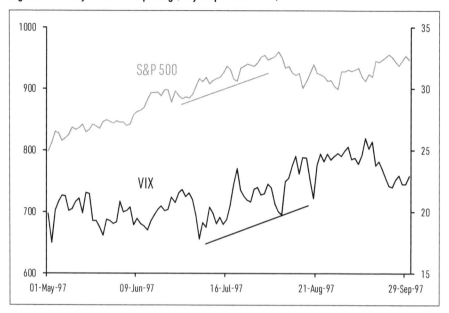

Data sources: Bloomberg and Cboe Global Markets.

The US stock market did not take much notice of the situation with respect to the Thai baht. On July 2 the S&P 500 rose by almost 1.5%. The markets were not as globally intertwined in 1997 as they are today. VIX was lower that day as well, moving from 21.00 to 19.70. However, note the trend lines in Figure 11.5. The S&P 500 continues to move higher, but after early July, VIX continues to trend higher as well. VIX represents the demand for SPX options and that demand was rising as the S&P 500 worked higher for a few weeks after the drop in the baht.

The S&P 500 shrugged off the news out of Asia, but derivative traders seemed to become a bit more concerned with respect to the direction of the S&P 500.

The crisis spread through South East Asia over the following weeks and eventually impacted developed stock markets. The October 27 drop in the S&P 500 was not necessarily the result of a single event and was attributed to high stock market valuations combined with concerns about US corporate earnings in the face of the crisis in Asia. Figure 11.6 shows the daily price action for VIX and SPX for the final three months of 1997.

Figure 11.6: Daily VIX and SPX pricing (October–December 1997)

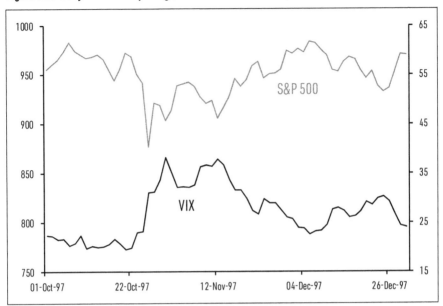

Data sources: Bloomberg and Cboe Global Markets.

VIX does not always give a contrarian signal before a drop in the equity markets. The price action around late October 1997 shown in Figure 11.6 is a perfect example of this. VIX made a new recent low the week before the drop on October 27. VIX also moved up as the S&P 500 rebounded after the drop—price action that would usually be associated with traders being concerned about further weakness in the S&P 500. By mid-November, VIX and the S&P 500 resumed their traditional inverse relationship as the market moved beyond the crisis.

OBSERVATIONS

The Federal Reserve did react to the stock market drop by lowering interest rates. This is a tool that has been used in reaction to crises long before the financial crisis of 2008. Although the world was a riskier place due to the Asian flu, VIX moved back down as the stock market was calmed by an early version of the Fed Put.

The price action of VIX and SPX during the summer as the crisis unfolded was a good early indication that traders were a bit concerned about what was going on in South East Asia as the cost of insuring a portfolio was rising despite the S&P 500 moving higher.

Asian flu sources: Trading Analysis of October 27 and 28, 1997 A Report by the Division of Market Regulation U.S. Securities and Exchange Commission September 1998.

RUSSIAN FINANCIAL CRISIS, AUGUST TO OCTOBER 1998

The Asian flu in 1997 was a precursor to what became known as the Russian Financial Crisis in 1998. This crisis was a series of events that resulted in Russia defaulting on their debt. Issues in Asia led to weakened demand for oil, which has a negative impact on the Russian economy. There were several other issues that plagued the economy as well, such as the cost of a war and strikes. About a month before Russia defaulted on its bonds, the IMF and World Bank put together a financial package worth over $20 billion. This still was not enough to avoid default. As an interesting side note, it has been suggested that $5 billion of the aid package was stolen upon arrival in Russia.

The demise of Long-Term Capital Management (LTCM) was one of the side effects of the Russian Financial Crisis. LTCM was a highly leveraged hedge fund that engaged in a type of spread trading that tried to capitalize on the divergence in performance between similar securities or markets. The firm was already experiencing poor performance, but the situation in Russia was likely the final straw that pushed the firm into a position that required a bailout from a consortium of Wall Street firms.

The first half of 1998 was pretty uneventful for the stock market, as shown in Figure 11.7. The S&P 500 was up over 10% in the first few months and then it was rangebound from April to June.

Something that does stand out in this chart is the quick moves to the upside for VIX when the S&P 500 traded off. For instance, on April 27, 1998 the S&P 500 lost 1.9% in a single day and VIX spiked from 21.97 to 26.09. Also, in mid-June the S&P 500 was down 3.3% between June 5 and June 15, which pushed VIX from 19.78 to 25.94. This could be taken as an early sign that despite a nice return for the S&P 500 in the first half of the year, market participants were a bit nervous with respect to the health of the stock market.

Figure 11.7: Daily VIX and SPX pricing (January–June 1998)

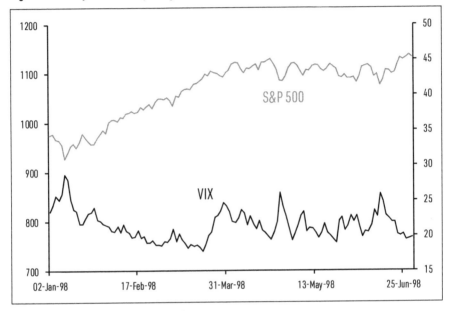

Data sources: Bloomberg and Cboe Global Markets.

Figure 11.8 shows the daily price action for the S&P 500 and VIX over the three-month period from July through September 1998. A steady downtrend in stocks and uptrend in VIX highlights that as the S&P 500 was dropping, there was still demand for portfolio protection in the form of SPX options. From July 17 to August 25 the S&P 500 lost about 8%, which drove VIX higher over that same period of time.

Figure 11.8: Daily VIX and SPX pricing (July–September 1998)

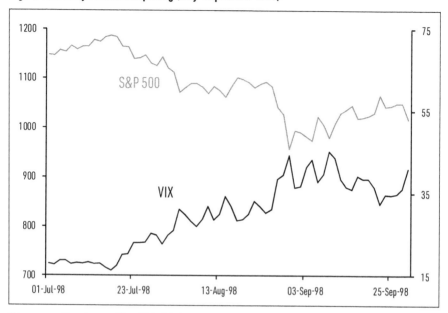

Data sources: Bloomberg and Cboe Global Markets.

The most dramatic drop during this period occurred from August 25 to August 31, when the S&P 500 gave up 12.4% and VIX responded by rallying to 44.28. August 31 marked the lowest close for the S&P 500 over the rest of 1998, but not the highest close for VIX. That came on October 8, when VIX closed at 45.74 on a day where the S&P 500 lost 1.16%, closing at 959.44, just above where the S&P 500 finished the day on August 31. Testing the market low from the last day in August may have created a feeling that another dramatic downside move for stocks was on the horizon.

Figure 11.9 highlights the price action over the last four months of 1998. After flirting with a new 1998 closing low, the S&P 500 moved up by 28.2% from October 8 through the end of the year. Over this same time period, VIX worked lower, but never closed below 20.00 through the end of 1998.

Figure 11.9: Daily VIX and SPX pricing (September–December 1998)

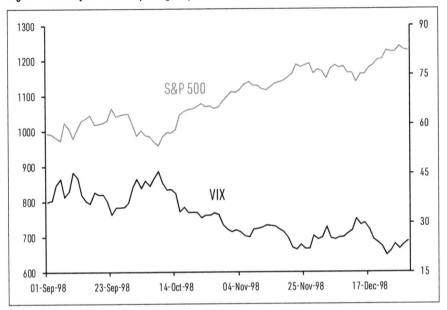

Data sources: Bloomberg and Cboe Global Markets.

OBSERVATIONS

A major observation of this volatility event is how it unfolded over the course of a couple of months in the price action of the S&P 500 and VIX. From July 17 to August 25, the S&P 500 lost about 8% and VIX rose from 16.23 to 30.33. The nature of the drop in the S&P 500 was pretty orderly, with only two days experiencing an S&P 500 loss of over 2%.

The annualized realized volatility over this period of time was about 20%. Despite realized volatility around 20%, VIX rose to a level over 30. This shows that VIX was anticipating a larger move in the near future. VIX got the direction right, but understated the subsequent realized volatility by about 10%.

Figure 11.10 shows the S&P 500 realized volatility for the 21 trading days following daily VIX closes. Note that VIX worked higher, which correctly indicated that the markets were starting to prepare for excess volatility. Despite almost doubling, VIX still underestimated what was to come.

Figure 11.10: Daily VIX closing prices and subsequent S&P 500 21-day realized volatility

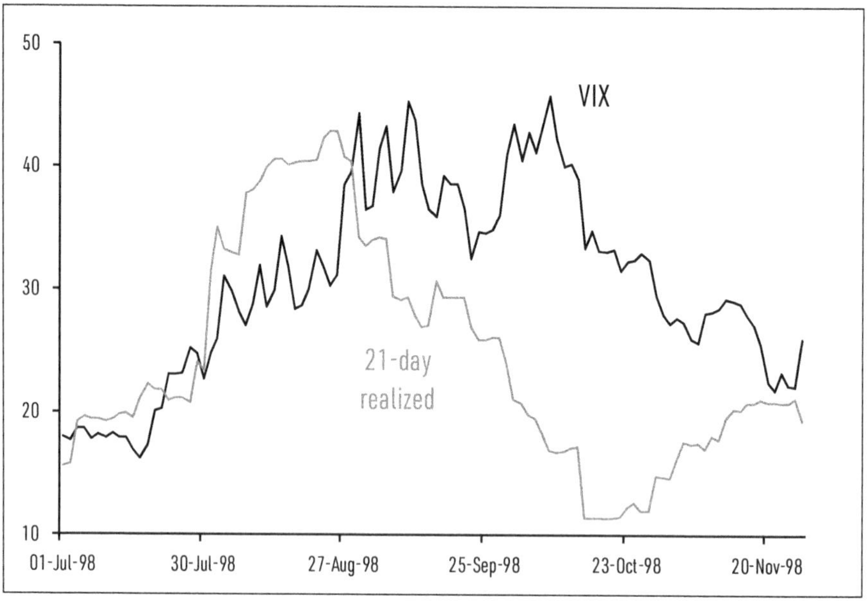

Data sources: Bloomberg and Cboe Global Markets.

One other interesting aspect of this chart is that once VIX spiked up to 44, coinciding with the end of a 12% drop in the S&P 500 over a short period of time, the index then overpriced the subsequent realized volatility for the rest of 1998.

Russian Financial Crisis Sources: Hirschler, Richard, ed. (August 1999). "Foreign Loans Diverted in Monster Money Laundering." World Bank – Transition. Lowenstein, Roger (2000). *When Genius Failed: The Rise and Fall of Long-Term Capital Management.* Random House.

SEPTEMBER 11, 2001 TERRORIST ATTACKS

The 9/11 terrorist attacks were a political event, but also a Wall Street event that had a direct impact on the financial markets due to the destruction of several buildings in Lower Manhattan. The attack hit the investment industry especially hard. The stock market in the US did not open on September 11, 2001 as the attacks commenced before the stock market's official opening time of 9:30 am. The stock markets resumed trading on September 17, 2001. Figure 11.11 covers the time period just before and just after the terrorist attacks.

Figure 11.11: Daily VIX and SPX pricing (July–October 2001)

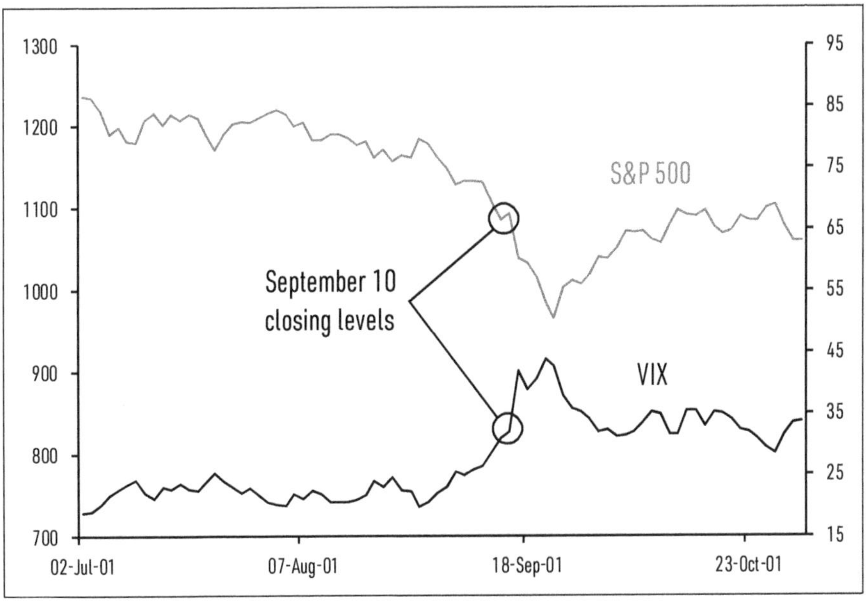

Data sources: Bloomberg and Cboe Global Markets.

The stock market was already experiencing some pressure and VIX was moving higher before the attacks. On September 10, the S&P 500 closed at 1092.54 and VIX finished the day at 31.84. When the markets reopened on September 17, the S&P 500 finished the day down by about 5% and VIX moved up to 41.76. The S&P 500 continued to move lower over the next few days, bottoming out on September 21 at 965.80, down by 11.6%. VIX actually topped out the day before (September 20) at 43.74.

OBSERVATIONS

In July and August 2001, VIX was rangebound, mostly closing between 19 and 25 over these two months. Following the attack there was a period of time, lasting most of the month of October, where VIX closed between 30 and 35. As some normalcy started to return to the United States, VIX adjusted its range again to around 21 to 26 for the remainder of 2001. This is shown in Figure 11.12, where each of these three rangebound periods are highlighted with support and resistance lines.

Figure 11.12: Daily VIX closing prices (July 2–December 31, 2001)

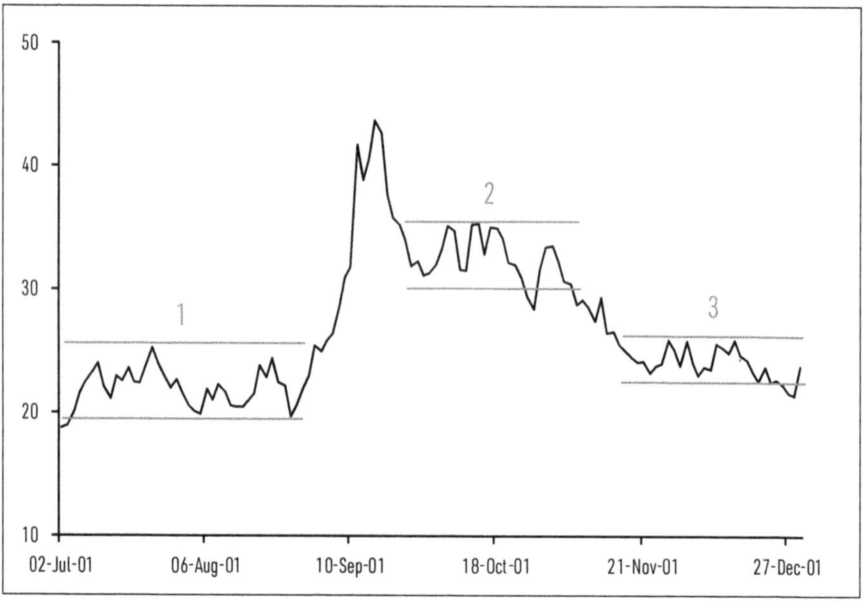

Data sources: Cboe Global Markets.

Market watchers who pay attention to VIX often refer to VIX indicating a high or low volatility regime. This definition is often pretty subjective and usually defined by what would be thought of as VIX being "high" or "low." The periods before and after the 9/11 attacks are a good example of VIX moving from one regime to another over the course of a few months.

GREAT FINANCIAL CRISIS, 2007-2009

The Great Financial Crisis (GFC) did not just suddenly happen in late 2008. There was a series of events that led up to the market volatility of late 2008 and early 2009. This period in market history is so important to volatility becoming an established tradable asset that it deserves three sections covering the market action before, during, and after the crisis.

LEADING UP TO THE GREAT FINANCIAL CRISIS, JANUARY 2007– SEPTEMBER 2008

It is always easy in hindsight to point out that the financial markets were indicating that a change in trend or sentiment was coming. However, looking at the behavior of VIX in 2007, there were some early indications that the stock market may be in for an increase in volatility. Figure 11.13 shows the price action for the S&P 500 and VIX for the full year 2007.

Figure 11.13: Daily VIX and SPX pricing (January–December 2007)

Data sources: Bloomberg and Cboe Global Markets.

The 2007 price action for the S&P 500 was pretty choppy and included three quick sell-offs over the course of the year, with two of those occurring during the final four months of the year. What is interesting is that the S&P 500 low for 2007 occurred in the first quarter while VIX was quoted higher during the incidents of market weakness in August and November.

During the March S&P 500 period of weakness, VIX did not even top 20. In both August and November VIX managed to close above 30. In 2007, VIX averaged 13.75 over the first seven months of the year. Over the final five months of the year the average VIX close was 22.71. Finally, note that there appears to be a shift higher for the range for VIX starting in August. All of these observations may be considered an indication that market participants were bracing for increased volatility.

The higher volatility range carried through to 2008. Figure 11.14 shows the market price activity over the first nine months of 2008. Again, in both January and March of 2008 VIX closed over 30, based on the S&P 500 coming under pressure.

Figure 11.14: Daily VIX and SPX pricing (January–September 2008)

Data sources: Bloomberg and Cboe Global Markets.

In April, VIX closed under 20 for the first time in 2008 and it appeared that VIX was on track to regress to a lower price range. By the summer, VIX began trending higher, with the S&P 500 trending lower, but it did dip below 20 one more time before events started to quickly unfold and led to what we now call the GFC.

GREAT FINANCIAL CRISIS, SEPTEMBER 2008–MARCH 2009

A slew of bad news started impacting financial markets during the final few months of 2008. Figure 11.15 highlights price action throughout 2008 which overlaps with the Figure 11.14. Including price action from all of 2008 does a better job of demonstrating just how dramatic the price action for both the S&P 500 and VIX was in the final months of 2008.

Figure 11.15: Daily VIX and SPX pricing (January–December 2008)

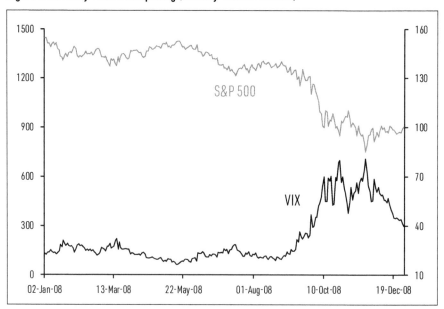

Data sources: Bloomberg and Cboe Global Markets.

VIX topped out on November 20, 2008 at 80.86. This was the all-time high for VIX until this figure was surpassed in 2020, with VIX closing high of 82.69. The very interesting aspect of the relative S&P 500 to VIX price action during the GFC was that VIX topped out in November, but the S&P 500 did not put in a final low until March 2009. Figure 11.16 covers the S&P 500 and VIX from September 2008 to March 2009.

Figure 11.16: Daily VIX and SPX pricing (September 2008–March 2009)

Data sources: Bloomberg and Cboe Global Markets.

From late November through the end of March, VIX appeared to trend in the same direction as the S&P 500. This has often been a precursor to a turnaround in the stock market, in both directions. However, from the VIX peak in November through the S&P 500 closing low of 676.53 on March 9, 2009, the price correlation between daily S&P 500 and VIX changes was −0.84. This is actually a greater negative correlation than during many other time periods.

POST-GREAT FINANCIAL CRISIS, MARCH TO DECEMBER 2009

The S&P 500 did not bottom out until March 2009 and then the stock market did nothing but trade higher for the balance of the year. In fact, traders that were lucky (there is no way anyone could attribute buying on this specific day to their being smart) enough to buy and hold something with S&P 500 exposure would have a return of about 65% just based on the price change for the S&P 500 from March 9, 2009 to the end of the year.

Figure 11.17 shows the price action for the full year 2009 for both VIX and the S&P 500.

Figure 11.17: Daily VIX and SPX pricing (January–December 2009)

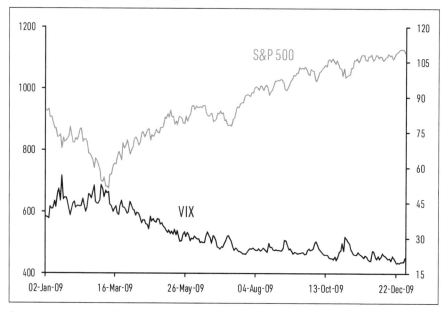

Data sources: Bloomberg and Cboe Global Markets.

Despite the huge bullish run for the S&P 500, VIX continued to remain at elevated levels. VIX averaged 28.37 for the balance of the year and also did not drop below 20 until December 22, 2009. Despite the strong price action for the S&P 500, VIX appears to indicate market participants remained on edge throughout most of 2009.

OBSERVATIONS

The GFC was the first sustained volatility event to occur after the introduction of VIX futures contracts. This was also the first time the VIX term structure remained in backwardation for a sustained period of time. Table 11.2 lists each instance where spot VIX closed higher than the front month future and the front month future was priced higher than the second month contract.

Table 11.2: VIX > Mo1 > Mo2 backwardation streaks

	VIX > Mo1 > Mo2			
Days	First day	Last day	VXX performance	S&P 500 performance
63	9/8/2008	12/10/2008	260.60%	−29.07%
35	2/24/2020	4/13/2020	130.39%	−14.39%
17	2/17/2009	3/11/2009	−2.40%	−8.59%
12	12/17/2018	1/3/2019	47.74%	−8.40%
11	1/6/2016	1/21/2016	14.81%	2.09%
11	10/18/2018	11/1/2018	14.93%	−3.67%
10	8/1/2011	8/12/2011	28.61%	−6.09%
10	8/17/2011	8/31/2011	5.57%	−1.03%
10	9/21/2011	10/4/2011	12.86%	−3.85%

Data source: Cboe Global Markets (the 2020 streak is still active and will be added to this table).

Prior to 2008 there had been no sustained period of time where the VIX term structure was in backwardation. At the opposite end of the spectrum, there are only two instances where the term structure was in backwardation for more than 20 trading days, during the GFC in 2008 and in response to the pandemic of 2020.

The GFC resulted in VIX reaching levels not seen since the predecessor to VIX, VXO, measured well over 100 during the crash of 1987. VIX topped out at 80.86 on November 20, 2008. Although this was the high for VIX, the GFC low for the S&P 500 was not established until March 9, 2009 at 676.53. This was 10% lower than the November closing level for the S&P 500 when VIX hit what was at the time an all-time high.

Figure 11.18: Daily VIX and SPX pricing (November 20, 2008–March 9, 2009)

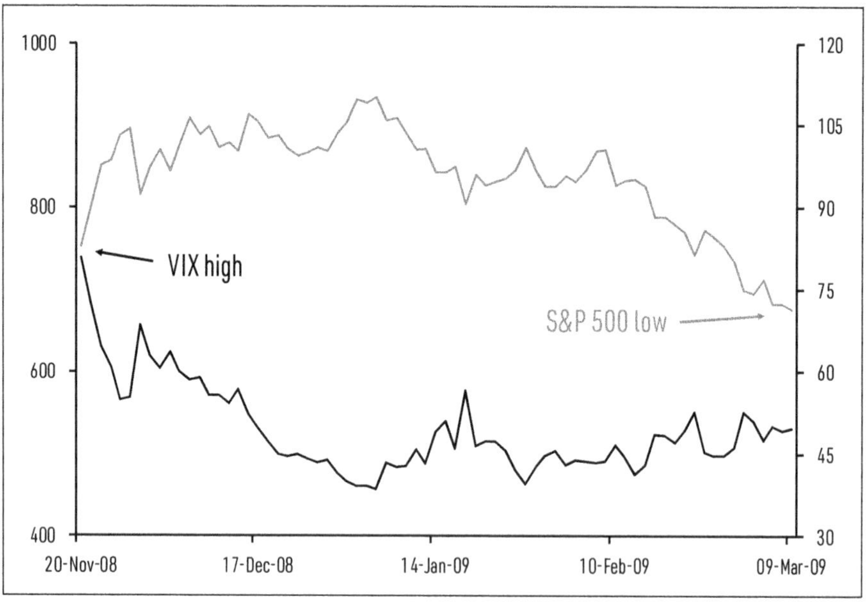

Data sources: Bloomberg and Cboe Global Markets.

A side effect of the VIX trading action in late 2008 was the establishment of the first two volatility-linked ETPs: VXX and VXZ. Volatility-linked ETPs have been a source of criticism for some time, as was discussed earlier in this book and will be addressed again later in this chapter. The day VXX launched, VIX was around 50.00, not exactly the best time to launch a long volatility product. Also worth noting is that VXX was created to match the performance of an index and there is performance data for this index going back to late 2005. Using this index as a proxy, VXX would have gained over 100% in October 2008.

FLASH CRASH, MAY 6, 2010

May 6, 2010 was a volatile day in the markets, with or without the trading action that became known as the flash crash. The flash crash occurred due to an S&P 500 E-mini futures order that was entered by a trader with Waddell & Reed out of Kansas City. The order was entered using an algorithm that was set up to sell 9% of the previous one-minute volume at the market. Because there was no limit, this order basically hit all bid prices over the course of just a few minutes. What exacerbated the issue was other systematic traders having to sell futures as well, which impacted S&P 500 stocks as well as other related derivatives.

Figure 11.19 shows the daily closing price action for spot VIX and the S&P 500 covering April through June of 2010. The closing prices for May 6, the day of the actual flash crash event, is highlighted for both VIX and SPX.

Figure 11.19: Daily VIX and SPX pricing (April–June 2010)

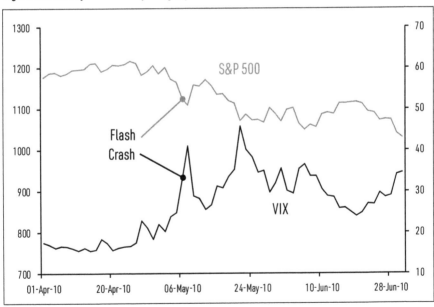

Data sources: Bloomberg and Cboe Global Markets.

The flash crash did not represent the closing high for VIX or closing low for the S&P 500 during this time frame. In fact, VIX closed higher on May 7 and the S&P 500 traded lower. There was a slight rebound, but then both VIX and S&P 500 moved to more extreme levels by the end of May. Eventually, in June the S&P put in lower closing lows. However, VIX did not move to higher levels than were seen in May, which was likely a function of the S&P 500 weakness being associated with a slow grind lower.

The flash crash covered a very short period of time, but had an impact that covered several weeks. The following figures give a better perspective of the flash crash than the previous daily chart. Figure 11.20 shows just how low the S&P 500 moved during the day on May 6. At the lowest point, the S&P index was down by 8.5%.

Figure 11.20: Daily S&P 500 index (May 3–May 14, 2010)

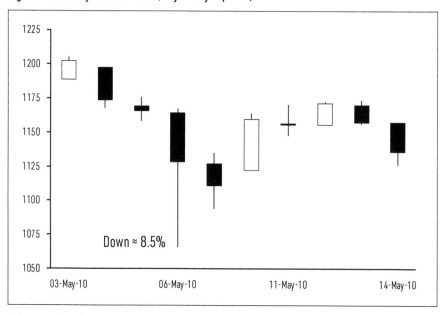

Data source: Bloomberg.

Remember, the flash crash was triggered by a trade error that occurred in the S&P 500 futures market. Figure 11.21 highlights the price action for those futures contracts around the day of the flash crash. Note the future moved down 9.3% while the spot index dropped 8.5%. The more dramatic drop in the futures would be expected since this is where the order was placed to push prices lower. At some point stock traders realized the individual equity prices were out of line with reality. This small human factor likely reduced the price impact on many individual stocks and the spot S&P 500.

Figure 11.21: Daily June 2010 S&P 500 future (May 3–May 14, 2010)

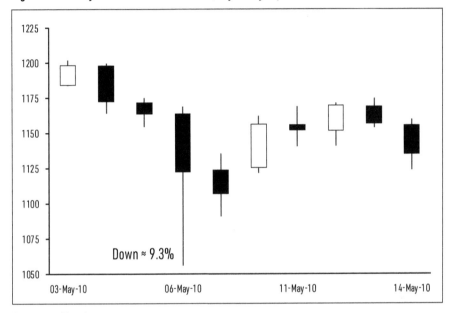

Data source: Bloomberg.

Figure 11.22 shows the price action for the VIX index around the period of the crash. Spot VIX moved up as much as 63% on the day, for a very short period of time, but closed lower than this, at 31.7% higher on the day.

Figure 11.22: Daily Spot VIX index (May 3–May 14, 2010)

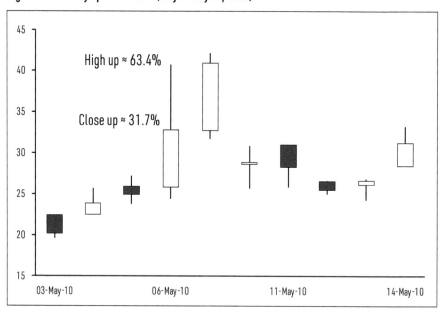

Data source: Bloomberg.

The May 2010 VIX future daily price action on the days surrounding the flash crash appears in Figure 11.23. The futures ran up more than spot VIX, rising 68% from the previous day's close during the brief uncertainty that accompanied the flash crash. The contract did manage to move down more dramatically from this high level to close the day up around 21%.

Figure 11.23: Daily May 2010 VIX future (May 3–May 14, 2010)

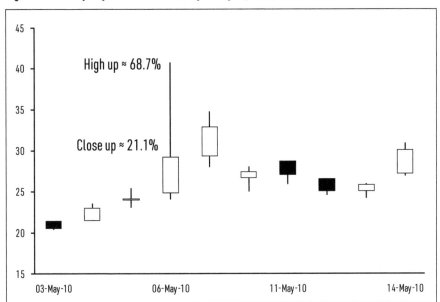

Data source: Bloomberg.

Figure 11.24 is a price study using the closing prices for spot VIX and the May future from April 22, 2010 through May 18, 2010. These days represent the closing price for each covering the time period where the May 2010 contract is the front month VIX future.

Figure 11.24: Daily VIX future and VIX index (May 2010)

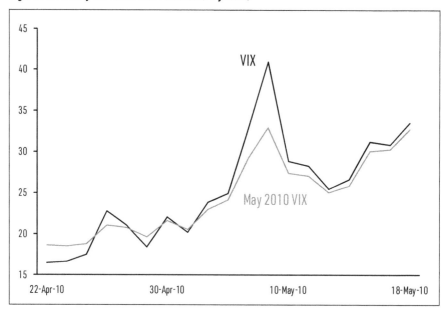

Data sources: Bloomberg and Cboe Global Markets.

In Figure 11.24 we can see that the May contract did not run up in sync with the May 7 price behavior for spot VIX. The future closed at 32.95 while spot VIX finished the day at 40.95. At this point there were seven trading days remaining until the May VIX future's expiration date. The following day, and throughout the remaining life of the May contract, the price action of spot VIX and May VIX moved in line with each other.

OBSERVATIONS

The most interesting aspect of the price action associated with the flash crash relates to what happened after the event. The flash crash was basically caused by a single trader making a very big mistake that caused a short-term (one hour) dislocation in asset prices. However, the range for VIX remained elevated for several months after the flash crash incident.

EUROPEAN SOVEREIGN DEBT CRISIS, 2011

The European sovereign debt crisis that arose in 2011 can be traced back to issues from the GFC in 2008–2009. Many EU countries were having issues with high deficits in the face of slowing economic activity. The result of these two factors was rising interest rates and concerns that some EU countries may default on their sovereign debt. Also, in May 2010 Greece received a bailout package that led many market participants to believe that other EU countries may be in trouble as well. It was noted in the previous section that VIX remained elevated after the flash crash in May 2010. The Greek bailout may have been a contributing factor to the elevated volatility expectations that remained in the market post-May 2010.

In the US, these issues eventually resulted in concerns that a repeat of the market activity experienced in 2008 was on the horizon in 2011. Figure 11.25 shows the price action leading up to the volatility spike associated with these concerns.

Figure 11.25: Daily VIX and SPX pricing (April–July 2011)

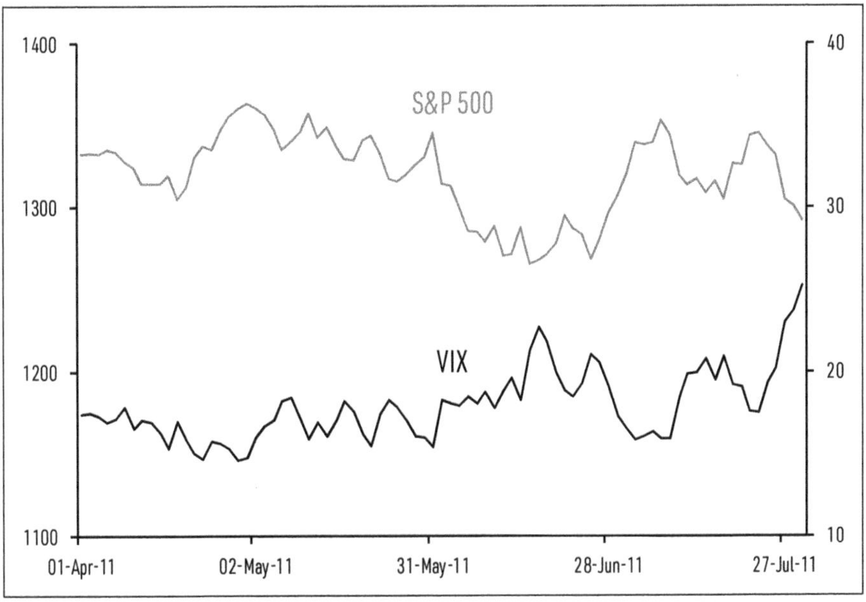

Data sources: Bloomberg and Cboe Global Markets.

From April 2011 through the middle of July, the range for VIX was 15 to 21. There were a couple of brief moves over 20 that subsided fairly quickly. However, toward the end of July, VIX started ramping up as the S&P 500 sold off. An interesting aspect to this price action is that VIX was making a new short-term high while the S&P 500 did not break through the closing lows from June 2011. Looking back, this was an indication of lower S&P 500 prices and higher VIX.

Figure 11.26 overlaps a bit with the previous figure, with both charts incorporating price action from July 2011. The data in Figure 11.26 runs through the end of 2011.

Figure 11.26: Daily VIX and SPX pricing (July–December 2011)

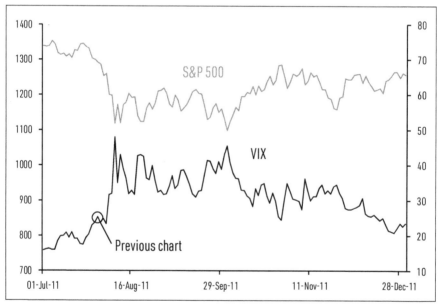

Data sources: Bloomberg and Cboe Global Markets.

The final data point from Figure 11.25 is highlighted in Figure 11.26 to show that even with a quick move higher, VIX will periodically continue to follow through to much higher levels. On the final day of July, VIX closed over 25, up over 30% in a five-day period. However, there was much more to go as the sovereign debt situation in Europe continued to develop. Only six trading days later VIX topped out at 48.00, 90% higher than the end of July close.

The final move up, on August 8, was a 50% day where VIX moved from 32.00 the previous day.

The crisis began in Europe and the Euro STOXX 50 Volatility Index (VSTOXX) was moving higher before the news started to impact US markets. Figure 11.27 recaps VIX and VSTOXX price action from April 2011 to July 2011.

Figure 11.27: Daily VIX and VSTOXX pricing (April–July 2011)

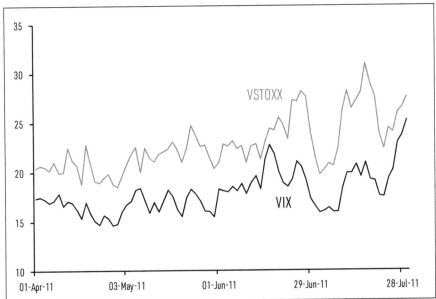

Data sources: Cboe Global Markets and Eurex Exchange.

VSTOXX is usually priced higher than VIX and both tend to trend in the same direction. Note that VSTOXX was putting in higher levels in July while VIX did not eclipse the closing high in June. This may have been an early indication that European market participants were more concerned about the future prospects for stocks than US traders. By the end of July, concerns showed up in VIX as it surpassed the first move to the upside like VSTOXX did earlier that month. Figure 11.28 shows VSTOXX and VIX price activity for July through October.

Figure 11.28: Daily VIX and VSTOXX pricing (July–October 2011)

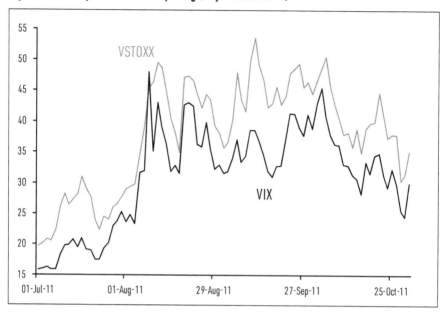

Data sources: Cboe Global Markets and Eurex Exchange.

In early August, as the sovereign debt situation in Europe impacted global markets, VIX quickly caught up with VSTOXX. On August 8, VIX closed slightly higher than VSTOXX. VIX moved down after peaking on August 8, but note that VSTOXX moved to higher levels and VIX eventually put in another move above 40.00. When things began to calm down in the markets, toward the end of Figure 11.28, both VSTOXX and VIX were moving lower together.

OBSERVATIONS

This was the first period of sustained higher VIX levels since the GFC and the first time many traders had exposure to VIX futures or ETPs during a volatility event (though VIX futures were available for trading during the 2008–2009 crisis). Many lessons were learned about what VIX and the associated trading vehicles do during periods of higher volatility. Figure 11.29 shows the August 2011 VIX future and spot VIX prices from July 20 to August 16. These dates were chosen as these are the days when the August contract was the front month future.

Figure 11.29: Daily VIX and Aug VIX pricing (July 20–August 16, 2011)

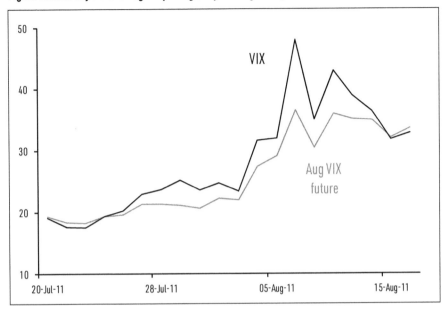

Data sources: Cboe Global Markets.

The August contract was trading at a slight premium to spot VIX for just a couple of days before VIX began to move up to close over 25.00 to end July. Note that the future remained at a discount to VIX until just before the August contract expired. There are two lessons here. First, it can be difficult and dangerous to short VIX futures on the first spike higher. Especially when the future is at a discount.

The second is that buying VIX futures if there is a belief that another leg to the move higher in VIX is coming soon can be a pretty safe trade. In Figure 11.29 there is actually a period of time where VIX moved down slightly and the future gained in price. On July 29, VIX closed at 25.25 while the August future closed at 21.10. On August 3, five trading days later, spot VIX was down 1.87 to 23.38 while the August future was up 0.65 to 22.00.

This was also the first sustained period with higher VIX that many VIX ETP traders experienced. Figure 11.30 shows the performance for the Aug VIX future, spot VIX index, and VXX from July 20 to August 16. The performance is indexed to 100 to better demonstrate the relative performance of each during this time period.

Figure 11.30: Aug VIX, VIX, and VXX performance (July 20–August 16, 2011)

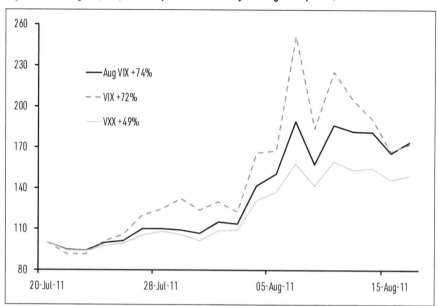

Data sources: Cboe Global Markets and Bloomberg.

Over this period of time, the August VIX future and spot VIX performance are basically in sync with each other. VXX would have returned 49%, still a healthy return, but trailing the other three instruments. The lesson here was for holders of VXX who were a bit frustrated at the underperformance of VXX relative to spot VIX and the VIX future. VXX's exposure to the September future, which rose by 28% over this time period, put a drag on VXX performance.

CHINA DATA AND BLACK MONDAY, 2015

In late August 2015, the markets experienced the biggest volatility event in years. The news from the Chinese markets had kept global markets on edge during the summer of 2015. Note in Figure 11.31, which shows the price action over the first seven months of 2015, that there is a small bout of higher volatility and lower stock prices that occurred around late June and early July 2015. However, the markets remained relatively calm until August 24.

Figure 11.31: Daily VIX and SPX pricing (January–July 2015)

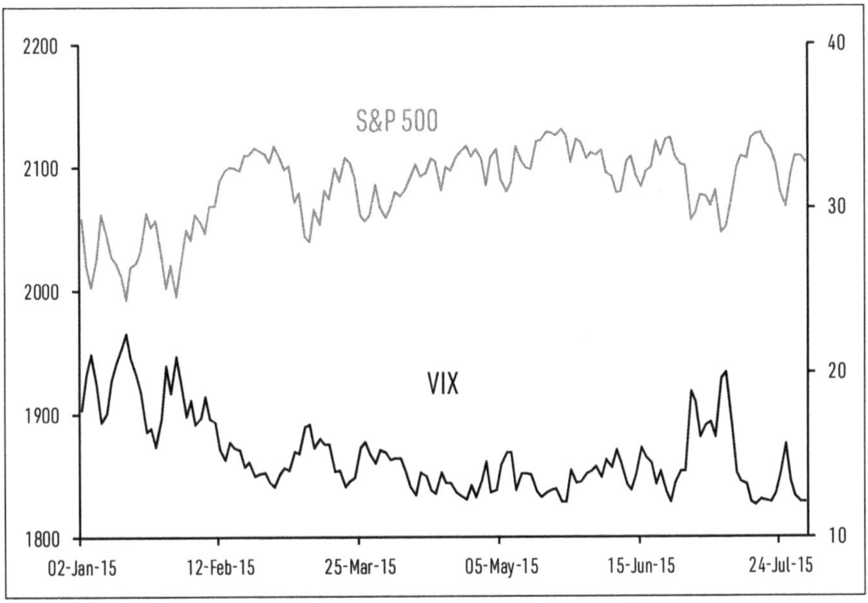

Data sources: Cboe Global Markets and Bloomberg.

Figure 11.32 shows the final five months of 2015 trading activity. The first three weeks of August were pretty normal and gave no real hint of what was to come.

Figure 11.32: Daily VIX and SPX pricing (August–December 2015)

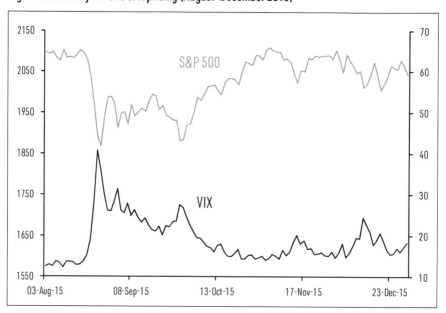

Data sources: Cboe Global Markets and Bloomberg.

The quick move higher in VIX and drop in the S&P 500 on Monday, August 24, demonstrates just how off-guard the financial markets were leading up to this day. VIX did start to show some signs of concern late on the previous Friday, with VIX moving up to 28. It then closed over 40 on August 24. The three-day price change for VIX ending on August 24 was the largest three-day move on record at the time.

Figure 11.32 is also a classic example of VIX not running to new highs when the S&P 500 is testing new lows. As the S&P 500 worked lower, VIX remained much lower than the August 24 high. This is the sort of price action that traders who use VIX as an indicator look for when assessing whether stocks are close to making a near term low.

OBSERVATIONS

This is another instance where VIX futures initially did not buy into the move. Figure 11.33 shows the price action for the September 2015 VIX future and spot VIX index from August 19, 2015 to September 15, 2015, the dates that the September contract was the front month VIX future.

Figure 11.33: Daily VIX and Sep VIX pricing (August 19–September 15, 2015)

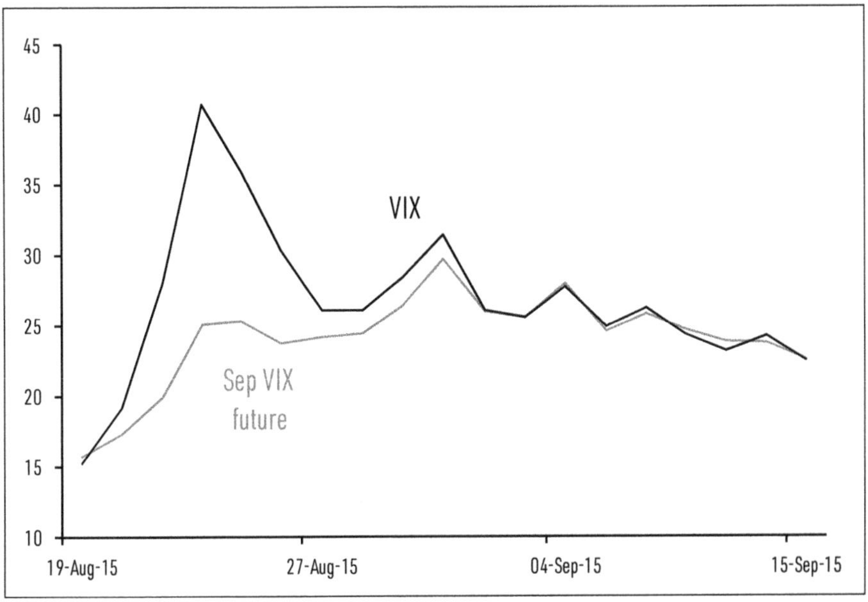

Data source: Cboe Global Markets.

The September VIX future settlement price on August 24 was 25.125, while VIX closed at 40.74. This discount of 15.615 is the largest closing spread between spot VIX and the front month future outside of the Great Financial Crisis and the pandemic of 2020. For several years, dating back to the price action in 2011, every VIX spike was followed by a quick move lower and this dramatic discount was influenced by this price action. Traders were not buying VIX futures despite the quick run up in the index. Also, there were 16 trading days remaining until the September VIX future expired, which gave VIX plenty of time to move back to more normal levels.

BREXIT REFERENDUM, 2016

The repercussions from the United Kingdom referendum in 2016—commonly referred to as Brexit—are still playing out. The outcome was surprising because the expectation was that the outcome would involve the UK remaining as a part of the European Union. We all know now that was not the outcome. The before and after reactions from VIX, VIX futures, and VSTOXX were an excellent example of how a regional event impacts volatility expectations of a local market and how, once the event spreads to become a focus in the US, VIX catches up very quickly.

Before looking at the price action of the indexes, an example of volatility traders getting something wrong is worth exploring. The outcome of the Brexit referendum occurred in the evening hours of June 23, 2016, after the VIX futures market had closed for the regular session. Figure 11.34 shows the term structure for spot VIX and the VIX futures contracts on June 23. The VIX front month VIX future closed at a slight discount to spot VIX.

Figure 11.34: Closing VIX term structure (June 23, 2016)

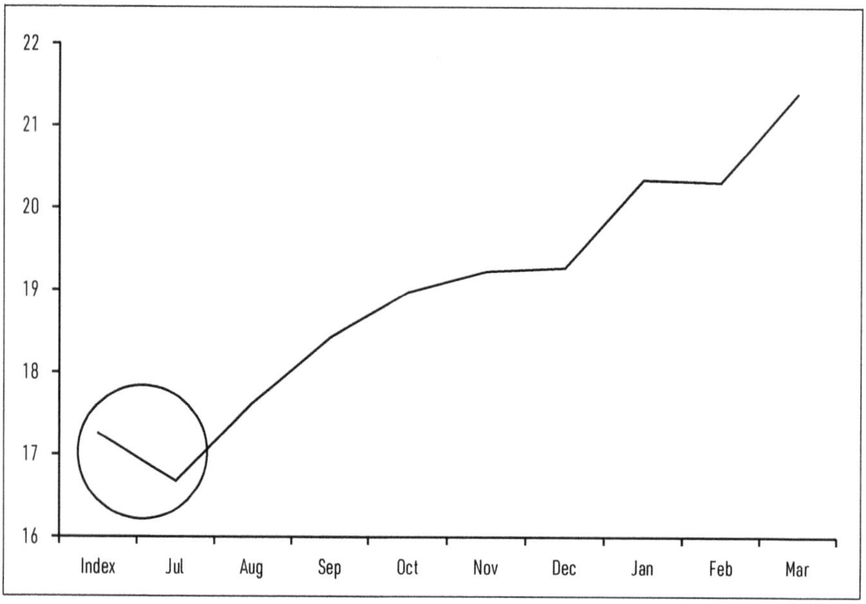

Data source: Cboe Global Markets.

Recall that VIX futures pricing takes into account a risk premium associated with being short volatility, along with a forecast for spot VIX. This is a rare example of the futures taking into account an actual event that is expected to calm fears and push VIX lower. The outcome that would result in VIX moving lower would be a rejection of the Brexit referendum. We all know that is not how the vote turned out.

Figure 11.35 shows the S&P 500 and VIX price action for May and June 2015. Note the market reaction to the Brexit outcome was negative for stocks and positive for uncertainty.

Figure 11.35: Daily VIX and SPX pricing (May–June 2016)

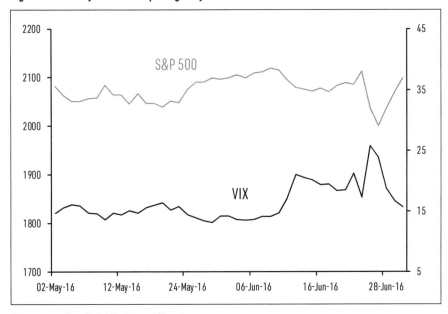

Data sources: Cboe Global Markets and Bloomberg.

In trading activity on June 23, the day of the vote and before the Brexit outcome was known, the S&P rose by 1.3% and VIX was down 3.92 to 17.25. This is definitely not the type of price action expected the day before a referendum that could disrupt global commerce. Of course, that is unless the markets were expecting the Brexit proposal would fail.

Figure 11.36 shows price action for June and July 2016 and the remarkable reaction by the US markets to the Brexit outcome. This is a textbook example of a 'V' market bottom with the S&P 500 rebounding after putting in a closing low on Monday, June 27.

Figure 11.36: Daily VIX and SPX pricing (June–July 2016)

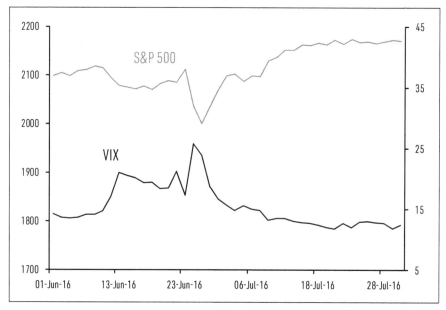

Data sources: Cboe Global Markets and Bloomberg.

Within a couple of weeks, the S&P 500 retraced losses associated with Brexit and VIX moved lower as well. In fact, by the end of July the S&P 500 was higher than June's highs, and VIX spent most of July closing lower than the June lows. This reaction was a function of the markets beginning to realize that the Brexit process was going to take a very long time and not impact commerce in the near term.

OBSERVATIONS

The impact of the Brexit referendum is a larger issue for European businesses than companies in the US. Figure 11.37 shows price action for the European version of VIX, VSTOXX, during the month of June versus VIX.

Figure 11.37: Daily VIX and VSTOXX index pricing (June 2016)

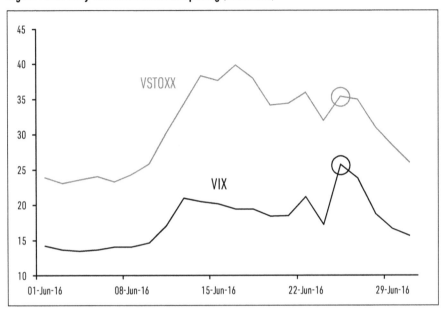

Data sources: Cboe Global Markets and Eurex.

Note that the Brexit reaction day is highlighted for the VSTOXX and VIX. Also note that the reaction from VIX was much higher than that of VSTOXX. There was a narrowing of the spread between the two volatility indexes on the trading day after the Brexit result. The narrowing was a function of VIX catching up with VSTOXX. It can be assumed that if Brexit had been rejected VSTOXX would likely have fallen more than VIX in reaction to that more business-friendly outcome.

Figure 11.38 shows the same data as Figure 11.37, but uses the front month July VSTOXX and VIX futures pricing. If a trader were considering taking advantage of the wide spread between VSTOXX and VIX, the first place they would look is the respective futures markets.

Figure 11.38: Daily VIX and VSTOXX futures pricing (June 2016)

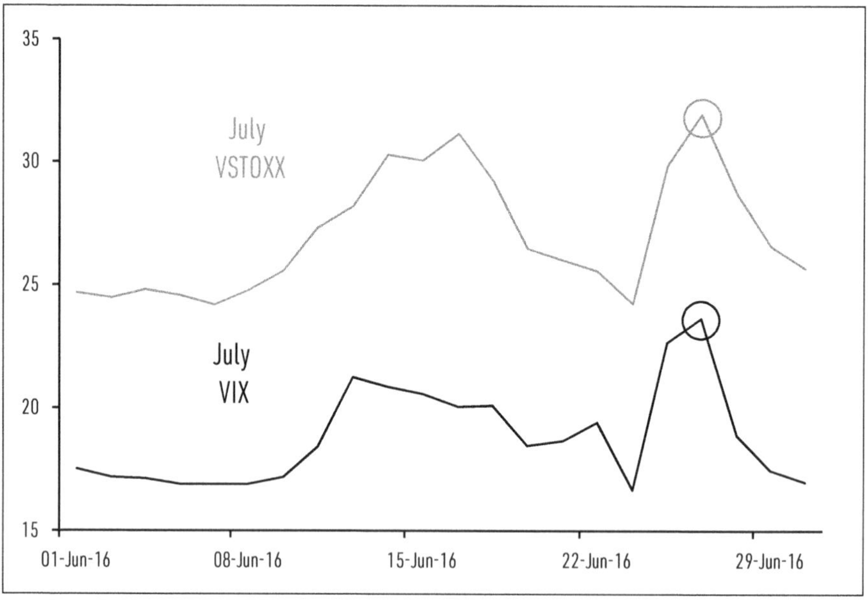

Data sources: Cboe Global Markets and Eurex.

The price reaction on June 24 is very similar for the VSTOXX and VIX futures contracts. July VSTOXX rose 5.60, while the July VIX future was up by 5.975. Basically, the spread between the futures narrowed, but not as much as the spread between the two indexes.

The divergence in the relative price action between the two is clearer in Figure 11.39, which shows the spread of the two indexes as well as the spread between the two futures contracts on a daily basis in June.

Figure 11.39: Daily VSTOXX over VIX index and futures spread (June 2016)

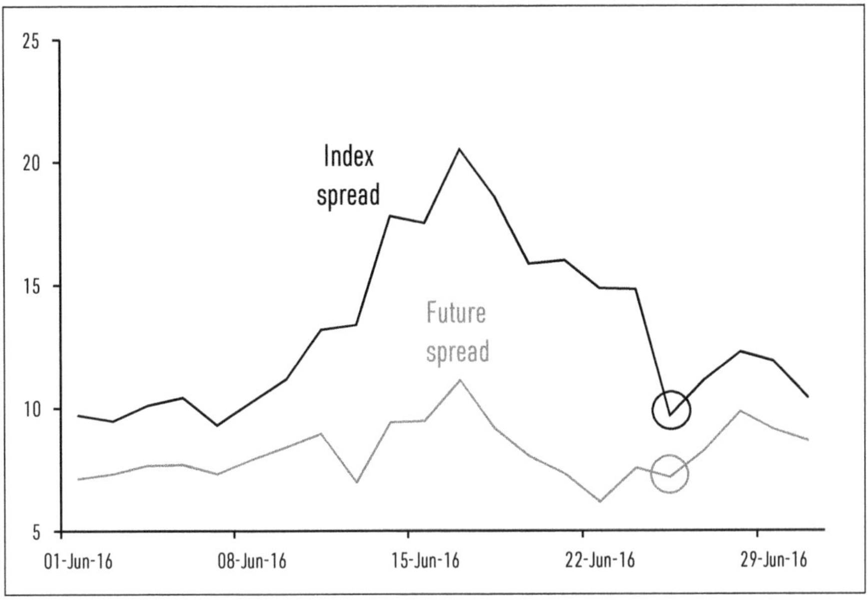

Data sources: Cboe Global Markets and Eurex.

Around events, near-term volatility futures price action should be given as much attention as the spot index, perhaps more. The futures market is where traders will put money to work based on an outlook, so this is what you need to be looking at. The spot index is affected by a fair value relationship and so it may not reflect a short-term outlook as well as the futures contract.

ELECTION OF DONALD TRUMP, 2016

Another surprising vote outcome was the election of Donald Trump as president of the United States in November 2016. It has been a long time since the outcome of the presidential election was different than the polls indicated. Typically, the markets in the US are not impacted too much in reaction to the presidential election, at least not like other markets around the world where election outcomes are more uncertain.

VIX and other volatility indexes appeared to be pricing in some risk going into the election. The results would be known, if it was not a disputed outcome, by November 9. VIX closed the day before at 18.74, up 0.03 on the day. This is a higher than average level for VIX, but was down from a recent high of 22.51 on November 4. Figure 11.40 highlights the pre-election VIX high as well as the reaction on November 9.

Figure 11.40: Daily VIX and SPX pricing (July–December 2016)

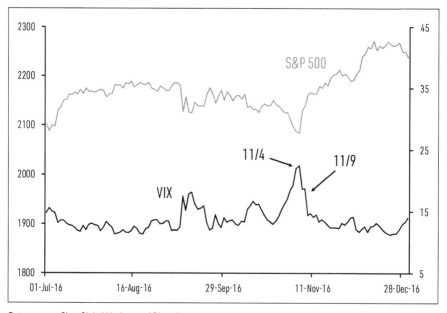

Data sources: Cboe Global Markets and Bloomberg.

The day after the election, VIX dropped by over 4 points to 14.38 and the S&P 500 was up by slightly over 1%. However, this is nowhere near the full story for VIX price action around the 2016 election.

VIX futures were actively traded as the results were coming in. Each time a battleground state was declared as won by Trump, VIX futures moved up more and S&P 500 futures moved lower. Once it became apparent that Donald Trump would be the next president of the United States, the S&P 500 futures hit limit down. VIX futures continued to trade and actually turned to the downside as S&P 500 futures began to recover. Figure 11.41 shows the price action from 5:00 pm to 9:00 am (Central time) the following morning in the December VIX and S&P 500 futures markets.

Figure 11.41: 5-minute pricing VIX and S&P 500 futures overnight on election night 2016

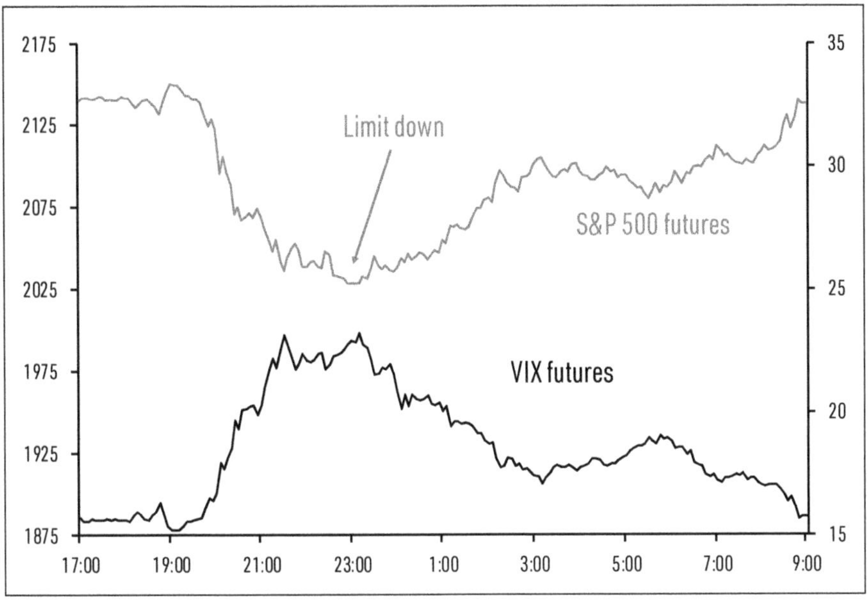

Data sources: Bloomberg.

The overnight price action for both the S&P 500 futures and VIX contracts was an incredible roller coaster. Cboe chose to keep VIX futures open while rules dictated that S&P 500 futures could not trade any lower for a short period of time. Market observers noted that the VIX future price started to drop before the S&P 500 futures rallied back to practically unchanged by the standard market open the next day.

OBSERVATIONS

There are several VIX-type indexes that cover different expectations for market volatility. Figure 11.42 shows the closing prices for nine-day (VIX9D), 30-day (VIX), three-month (VIX3M), and six-month (VIX6M) volatility indexes the Friday before and the Friday after the 2012 election. It is helpful to compare the market action around the 2012 election, because this was an election that had some more certainty and less fear surrounding the impact of the winner.

Figure 11.42: 2012 election week over week VIX9D, VIX, VIX3M, VIX6M term structure

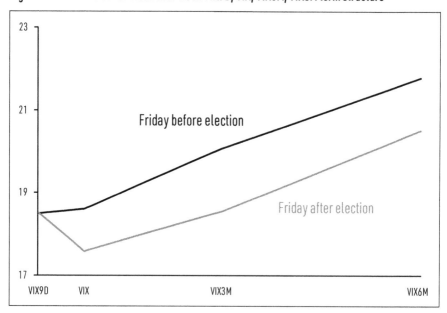

Data source: Cboe Global Markets.

Notice on the Friday before the election the nine-day volatility index was much higher than VIX. This can be taken as traders thinking we may be seeing a volatile week in the near term, but then things should calm down pretty quickly. After the election of 2012, relative volatility index prices moved back to what is considered a normal term structure.

The 2016 election was like no other in recent memory, and the volatility index price activity shows this as well. Figure 11.43 shows the same indexes as before. Note on the Friday before the election VIX9D was close to 30, VIX was also higher than the three-month volatility index. All of this is the type of relative volatility index price action that is associated with a higher-risk market. Usually this sort of price action is a reaction to news, not an anticipation of market-moving news.

Figure 11.43: 2016 election week over week VIX9D, VIX, VIX3M, VIX6M term structure

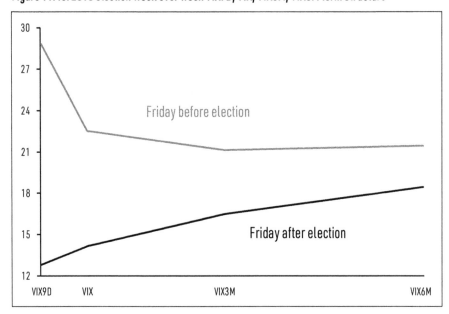

Data source: Cboe Global Markets.

Finally, note the post-election Friday curve. VIX was below 15 and the curve indicated very little anticipation of excess volatility that would be associated with the incoming administration.

Basically, all the fear and uncertainty associated with a Trump presidency occurred in the space of a few hours. The S&P 500 futures dropped 10% overnight and VIX futures were up 50% during the overnight session. By 9:00 am the next morning VIX futures were 0.05 higher than the price at 5:00 pm the night before. S&P 500 futures were only 2.00 points lower. Both markets experienced the type of price action that often takes months in a very short period of time.

There were a couple of takeaways from that night. First, VIX proved itself as a tradable market in the extended hours as the market set overnight volume records and handled more trading during what Cboe calls "extended trading hours." Also, the price action in the VIX and S&P 500 futures markets mirrored each other over the course of the night. The VIX future put in the session high while S&P 500 futures were trading limit down, and the move lower in VIX future appears to have preceded the recovery in S&P 500 futures. VIX showed itself as a good confirming indicator relative to the S&P 500 that evening.

INFLATION IN EMPLOYMENT NUMBER, FEBRUARY 2018

On the first Friday (generally) of each month the financial markets brace for the "employment number." Officially, the employment number is a broad array of data that is released at 8:30 am Eastern time by the Bureau of Labor Statistics. The business press mostly focuses on numbers like the unemployment rate and whether there was an increase or decrease in the number of nonfarm payroll employment.

The initial news that resulted in this volatility event came out on Friday, February 2, 2018. The S&P 500 ended up losing over 2% on that day, but VIX did not react as one would expect, closing at 17.31. The follow-through on February 5 is what gave us the term "Volmageddon."

VIX more than doubled in a single day, rising to 37.32 as the S&P 500 lost 4% on the day. The three-day rise for VIX, in percentage terms, was the biggest three-day move on record, up about 175%. Figure 11.44 shows the daily price action for the first three months of 2018.

Figure 11.44: Daily VIX and SPX pricing (January–March 2018)

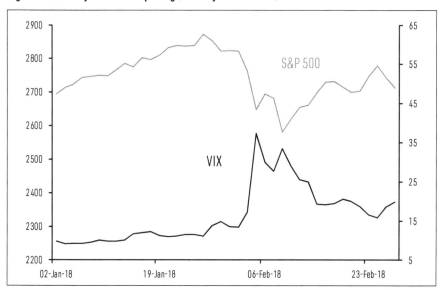

Data sources: Cboe Global Markets and Bloomberg.

The February 5 drop in the S&P 500 and subsequent spike in VIX to the upper 30s is very apparent on the chart. However, lost in the whole Volmageddon legend is that the S&P 500 made a new low just after the initial reaction. However, VIX did not confirm that move lower and offered up a signal that the market was not about to panic sell stocks again.

OBSERVATIONS

This incident was an unfortunate lesson for traders who had been attracted to short volatility strategies. Taking advantage of the consistent overpricing of VIX futures contracts had become a pretty popular strategy. Professionals were attracted to VIX futures and options while smaller traders gravitated to the ETPs that offered opposite exposure to that of products like VXX. VXX would consistently grind lower and the short volatility-related ETPs tended to perform quite well. The two biggest products at the time were the ProShares Short VIX Short Term Futures ETF (SVXY) and the VelocityShares Daily Inverse VIX Short Term ETN (XIV). On February 5 XIV, based on the NAV, experienced a loss of 96%. Figure 11.45 shows the daily NAV for XIV from January 2, 2018 to February 15, 2018.

Figure 11.45: Daily XIV pricing (January 2–February 15, 2018)

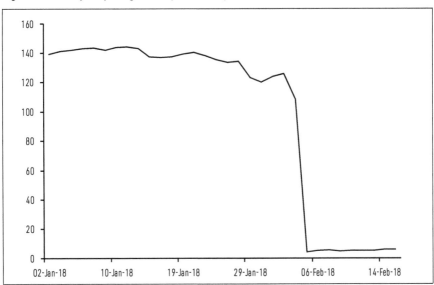

Data source: Bloomberg.

Figure 11.45 ends on February 15 because that's the day the issuer of XIV retired the ETN and returned whatever cash was left to holders on that day. SVXY suffered similar price action, but did not close and is still available for trading. However, SVXY deleveraged a bit, and now offers half the inverse daily performance of the strategy that VXX is long. This actually was a positive development, as during the market issues in 2020 SVXY lost about 56% when VIX futures were trading at elevated levels in mid-March.

GLOBAL PANDEMIC, 2020

In late 2019 the SARS-CoV-2 virus and associated disease COVID-19 started to spread around the world. By March 2020, the United States was affected and the result was a negative impact on the economy and financial markets.

The uncertainty associated with the economic impact of the pandemic resulted in the S&P 500 losing almost 34% over the course of 23 trading days. VIX reacted as expected and rose from under 15 to over 80 during this period of time. VIX reached levels that were previously only witnessed during the Great Financial Crisis. Figure 11.46 shows the daily price action for both the S&P 500 and VIX from November 2019 to May 2020.

Figure 11.46: Daily VIX and SPX pricing (November–May 2020)

Data sources: Cboe Global Markets and Bloomberg.

The price action is so dramatic over this time period that the lines representing the S&P 500 and VIX overlap. The closing high for VIX occurred on March 16, while the closing low for the S&P 500 during this time period happened one week later on March 23. The consistent trend lower for VIX and higher for the S&P 500 was probably reassuring to those who had bought stocks during this time period. However, in late May VIX started to flatten out in the mid-20s and that lack of continued downtrend started to become a bit concerning for market participants.

As VIX started to react to the growing pandemic story the VIX futures initially lagged the move by a large amount. The market was conditioned to spikes in VIX moving lower in a short period of time and the front month Mar VIX futures pricing in late February reflected this.

Figure 11.47 shows daily closing prices for the March future from February 3 to the March 18 contract settlement date.

Figure 11.47: Daily VIX and Mar VIX pricing (February 3–March 18, 2020)

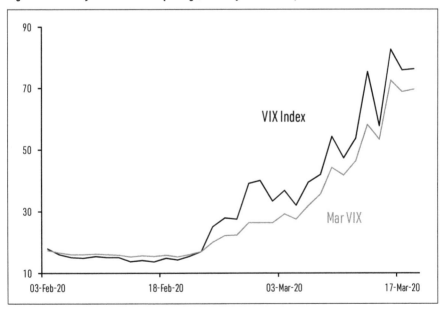

Data sources: Cboe Global Markets and Bloomberg.

Spot VIX closed higher than the March future on February 21 with VIX closing at 17.08 and the Mar VIX contract settling at 16.925. The following day, spot VIX was five points higher than the futures contract. On the last trading day of February, spot VIX topped 40, closing just over 13.50 points higher than the future. In time, the March contract would narrow the gap a bit, but never closed above spot VIX over the balance of the contract's life.

The April future behaved in a similar way, but was around as VIX started to move lower. Figure 11.48 shows the daily price changes for both spot VIX and the Apr VIX future from February 3 to April 13.

Figure 11.48: Daily VIX and Apr VIX pricing (February 3–April 13, 2020)

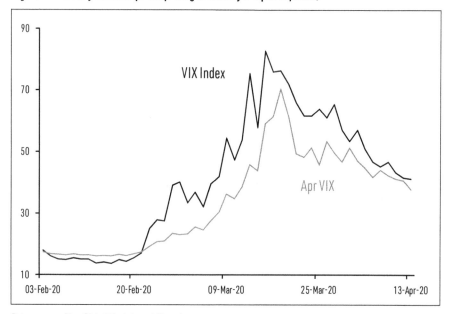

Data sources: Cboe Global Markets and Bloomberg.

Spot VIX closed higher than the April contract for the first time on February 24 and never closed at a discount through the life of the Apr VIX future. The future followed VIX higher and then changed direction in line with spot VIX, but always maintained a discount. Both the Mar VIX and Apr VIX futures contracts offered an opportunity to get long volatility as the story was developing—a rare occurrence—but something that should be considered when a trader believes a crisis is developing.

Although VIX Weekly options and futures have been around for some time, the volume is usually a small part of the daily volume for each market. However, during the pandemic one large trader used VIX Weekly options to take advantage of VIX at elevated levels by selling puts. In late February and early March there was a seller of well over 100,000 VIX Apr 1 23 puts at prices between 0.92 and 2.25. The VIX future that expired on April 1 was trading in the mid-20s when these options were sold. These positions were held through expiration with settlement for April 1 VIX futures and options coming in at 58.33, which resulted in a very nice profit for the seller of these puts. Over the course of a couple of weeks, the Apr 1 23 puts had the highest open interest of any VIX option contract, which was the first time a non-standard option was the biggest holding among VIX options.

A final, somewhat non-quantitative observation, is that the VIX complex remained open and provided sufficient liquidity throughout the worst part of the pandemic. Cboe closed their trading floor and made all VIX option trading electronic with the switch occurring over a weekend. Having worked at Cboe for several years, I am very aware of just how much effort went into maintaining this marketplace during a difficult period. Commentators like to complain about the financial industry when things go wrong, but I believe this is a moment where Cboe should be commended for navigating a very difficult time.

OBSERVATIONS

The first major observation is that VIX topped out at a level very close to the peak close during the Great Financial Crisis. Theoretically, VIX can reach much higher levels, but the 80s will be a price level that traders fixate on when the next volatility event hits the financial markets.

VIX topped out before the S&P 500 put in the ultimate low. This pattern seems to repeat during volatility spikes, where VIX peaks out before the S&P 500 makes a final low.

Finally, there was wide usage of non-standard VIX Weekly options which demonstrated that the VIX pit is available to offer liquidity when institutions are seeking out exposure to VIX options that expire on a non-standard date.

HISTORY LESSONS

There are many lessons from the behavior of VIX and the related markets during periods of elevated volatility expectations. Knowing history and actually having traded through it are two different scenarios, but it does help to have an awareness of what has happened in the past when facing volatility events in the markets. Here are a few things to always keep in mind.

- VIX can go higher—just because VIX has not been in the 20s for a year does not mean we will not suddenly see a 40 handle on spot VIX.

- The long volatility-related ETPs do what they are supposed to do when they are supposed to do it—meaning that they offer handsome returns over a short period of time during volatility events.

- VIX futures will not move up as quickly as spot VIX during the initial spike—VIX traders are conditioned to sell volatility and the result is VIX futures often lagging an upside move from spot VIX.

- Shorting volatility works until it doesn't—there will be periods where a short volatility position encounters a quick dramatic loss. Make sure there's some sort of risk control in place with any short VIX exposure.

Milton Keynes UK
Ingram Content Group UK Ltd.
UKHW020730210924
448482UK00004B/86